D0760789

Art of Celebration
SOUTHERN CALIFORNIA

Published by

PANACHE
PANACHE PARTNERS

Panache Partners, LLC
1424 Gables Court
Plano, TX 75075
469.246.6060
Fax: 469.246.6062
www.panache.com

Publishers: Brian G. Carabet and John A. Shand

Copyright © 2010 by Panache Partners, LLC
All rights reserved.

No part of this book may be reproduced or transmitted in any form or by any means, electronic or mechanical, including photocopying, recording or by any information storage or retrieval system, except brief excerpts for the purpose of review, without written permission of the publisher.

All images in this book have been reproduced with the knowledge and prior consent of the professionals concerned and no responsibility is accepted by the producer, publisher, or printer for any infringement of copyright or otherwise arising from the contents of this publication. Every effort has been made to ensure that credits accurately comply with the information supplied.

Printed in Malaysia

Distributed by Independent Publishers Group
800.888.4741

PUBLISHER'S DATA

Art of Celebration Southern California

Library of Congress Control Number: 2010927256

ISBN 13: 978-1-933415-93-2
ISBN 10: 1-933415-93-2

First Printing 2010

10 9 8 7 6 5 4 3 2 1

This publication is intended to showcase the work of extremely talented people. The publisher does not require, warrant, endorse, or verify any professional accreditations, educational backgrounds, or professional affiliations of the individuals or firms included herein. All copy and photography published herein has been reviewed and approved as free of any usage fees or rights and accurate by the individuals and/or firms included herein.

Panache Partners, LLC, is dedicated to the restoration and conservation of the environment. Our books are manufactured with strict adherence to an environmental management system in accordance with ISO 14001 standards, including the use of paper from mills certified to derive their products from well-managed forests. We are committed to continued investigation of alternative paper products and environmentally responsible manufacturing processes to ensure the preservation of our fragile planet.

Art of Celebration

SOUTHERN CALIFORNIA

FOREWORD

Having popularized the concept of eco-chic events, revolutionized the interactive quality of parties large and small, and set the bar unbelievably high for star-quality galas, it's more than fair to say that Southern California's event planning, design, and production professionals are thought-leaders across the industry. We are undaunted by the idea of entertaining thousands of Hollywood's most elite at the Oscars, Grammys, and Golden Globes—not to mention developing fresh new concepts to please familiar crowds from year to year.

The people whose work is featured within are an exciting mix of California natives with a global perspective and Golden State newcomers who possess an innate sensitivity to cultures and traditions of all sorts. For everything from film premieres to product launches to birthday parties, their talent is sought in local hot spots like Los Angeles, Palm Springs, and San Diego as well as around the world.

With such a global reach, it's no wonder that Southern California event professionals regularly appear on local and national television to offer expertise, and have even popped up on reality shows dedicated to the non-stop glamour and excitement of the event world. For each, however, it's a priority that every guest receives the star treatment whether their name appears above the title or simply on the invitation.

This extraordinary collection, *Art of Celebration Southern California*, reveals exclusive insider tips and tales from some of the most incredible parties in the world. With all this area has to offer—incredible natural scenery, a close proximity to Hollywood, and worldly, sophisticated residents—sometimes we have to pinch ourselves just to make sure we're really here.

Marc Friedland

INTRODUCTION

Celebrations are woven into our lives from the moment we are born; we pave our long and winding road with revelry. Cultures are identified by their milestones, rites of passage, and faiths. From the visions of a select few, through the work of many, and motivated by all, our life's celebrations are universal.

In *Art of Celebration Southern California*, we chart the area's modern-day visionaries who mastermind remarkable events, creating everlasting memories.

The magic of a phenomenal celebration is achieved with great collaboration. This book will take you on a journey, sharing the insights and creations of the gifted. We begin this journey with SOCIAL AND CORPORATE EVENT SPECIALISTS—the directors and producers—who pull it all together, manage and execute the visions. And because once you've set the date, the next step is LOCATION, LOCATION, LOCATION, we turn our focus to Southern California's most incredible venues, which become inspirational backdrops. From there, IT'S ALL IN THE DETAILS.

The event, floral, and lighting designers are true visionaries of CREATING AN AMBIENCE; these artists are responsible for the endless ideas and boundless efforts and are often the heart and soul of an unforgettable gala. Then EAT, DRINK & BE MERRY in the culinary world of caterers, whose works of art and ingenious creations delight the palate and astound the mind. Through the amazing talents of musicians, entertainers, and photographers, CAPTURING THE MOMENT will forever keep alive the experiences of life's ritual—the art of celebration.

Art of Celebration Southern California will inspire, inform, and just might take your breath away!

Carla Bowers
Senior Publisher

Social Event Specialists

Corporate Event Specialists

Location, Location, Location

It's All In the Details

CONTENTS

BEFORE THE MUSIC BEGINS...

Social Event

Specialists

Rrivre Works, Inc.

RRIVRE DAVIES

His resume reads like a Hollywood yearbook: Disney, Showtime, Miramax Films, HBO, Warner Bros., ESPN, Fox, Paramount, not to mention the Academy of Motion Picture Arts and Sciences and the Director's Guild of America. But no matter how large or small the event, Rrivre Davies and his team of Event Design Artisans™ are there from beginning to end, making sure that every single detail is exactly how it should be.

As the child of British and American parents, California native Rrivre spent most of his youth traveling the globe, visiting over 30 countries by the time he entered college. Since he grew up in Santa Barbara near the entertainment industry, it came as no surprise that Rrivre became an art director for films, commercials, and music videos. But when a friend asked him to create the décor for a premiere of Disney's "Pocahontas," Rrivre found himself working on an entirely new level—and loving it. Soon he was designing for all the Disney celebrations, and from there it only blossomed.

By employing a process called "3-D design," Rrivre can visually analyze an event space from every possible angle and adjust his design to maximize the visual and experiential emotional impact. Led by Vice President of Production Evaristo Martinez, the Event Design Artisans™ take Rrivre's concept and then produce high-quality and high-style event furnishings, drapery, cabanas, props and other décor elements before installing them for the event. Utilizing his love of travel, Rrivre can recreate any place as an event environment, whether it exists or not.

Designing a dinner party on the roof of Cartier posed two very big challenges: the space was long and narrow, and the elevators were too small to hold much equipment. To give the illusion of space I used a wider tent and pulled the sides in, which allowed me to add recesses and cut-outs. I also created a wall of silver-leaf-framed mirrors at each end of the tent. We hoisted everything up three stories with ropes! The transformation was so complete the president of Cartier asked us which one of his rooms we were standing in. Designed for Along Came Mary, floral by Eric Buterbaugh, lighting by Daylight.

Photograph by Dan Scott, American Image Gallery

Photograph by Parker J. Fister, parkerjphoto.com

Photograph by Parker J. Fister, parkerjphoto.com

Bringing the indoors outside is a popular design route, but sometimes the outdoor setting is so charming that it's better to play up its rustic, bucolic attributes. Beautiful arches bearing twinkling crystal and wrought-iron chandeliers surrounded the three dining areas, where elegant table linens and dishware kept the mood refined. To see guests in tuxedos and ball gowns, toasting marshmallows to make gourmet s'mores under the stars, made the night just magical. Designed for Sacks Productions, floral by Krislyn Design, lighting by Images by Lighting.

Photograph by Parker J. Fister, parkerjphoto.com

Above and facing page: With an event as dynamic as the Pre-BET party, you can't shoehorn people into traditional seating arrangements and expect them to be happy. S-shaped booths with intimate tables and ottomans, bar-height tables, and other avant-garde groupings ensured that guests could move around the room easily. Designed for Events by André Wells, chairs by Chameleon Chairs, floral by Eric Buterbaugh, lighting by ELS.

Left: Red roses and calla lilies are tried-and-true event flowers, but they get a punch from the innovative use of graphic black and white patterned balls. Floral by Gina Park-Mille Fiori.

Photograph by Marianne Lozano Photography

Photograph by Marianne Lozano Photography

Photograph by Marianne Lozano Photography

Photograph by Peter Jordan Photography

Photograph by Peter Jordan Photography

Photograph by Peter Jordan Photography

"I cannot think of a better career in the world than bringing beauty and joy to people's special and momentous occasions."

—Rrivre Davies

The "Hamptons Chic" 16th birthday party was every girl's—and woman's—dream come true. A combination of beach-inspired artifacts mixed with overstuffed furniture and stately columns more likely to be seen on a porch in the Hamptons helped achieve a shabby chic experience. An airy tent structure allowed for wrought-iron and shell-encrusted chandeliers to hang above the party, while flooring around the buffets transported guests onto an old-fashioned boardwalk. The columns the food was displayed upon were designed for versatility; the panels of fabric can be switched out to match any event's décor. Designed for Grand Affair, floral by Mindy Rice Floral Design.

Photograph by Peter Jordan Photography

Photograph by bb Photography

Photograph by bb Photography

"It's so invigorating and rewarding to see people's reactions when walking into a world that you created."
—Rrivre Davies

Left: After my sister and I left home, our parents turned the house we'd grown up in into the Simpson House Inn, North America's only Five Diamond bed-and-breakfast. It was there in Santa Barbara that I hosted a two-night retreat for event coordinators and was able to try out some ideas I'd been playing around with for a while. One thing I see time and again is people being confined to socializing for long periods with only those in their immediate area. To speak to someone new, you have to get up and leave your plate. For each course at this event, the dining areas were set up on different parts of the property, creating a moveable feast. For each course guests were encouraged to choose their own seats and converse with different people throughout the meal. Floral by Camilla Svensson Burns Floral Design, catering by Good Gracious! Events.

Facing page: Drawing inspiration from the things you love in everyday life is always a smart decision. A lavender and silver bedroom translated into a stylish and graceful reception area in the host's backyard. In an effort to avoid a standard draped tent ceiling, I devised a system where the fabric swathed the edges but collected into a tufted center, complete with a mirror at the very top. Floral by The Hidden Garden, lighting by Images by Lighting.

Photograph by Dan Scott, American Image Gallery

Photograph by Michael Simon, STARTRAKS

Photograph by Marianne Lozano Photography

"Events are the moments in life we create to remember, talismans of our lives and human history."
—Rrivre Davies

Right: When I was 15, I went to Morocco and completely fell in love with the intensity of the colors, patterns, and textures. My design may not be truly authentic, but my respect and adoration of the style comes through. Designed for TGIS.

Facing page: The marriage of reality star Khloe Kardashian and LA Laker Lamar Odom was a chance to showcase a design that was both hip and romantic. Contemporary seating, white suede tablecloths with black suede trim, and a white faux crocodile wall delighted guests. I love placing mirrors in tents, because not only do they reflect light, but they also bring a sense of constant movement, something that is often lost with the absence of windows. Designed for Sacks Productions, floral by Mark's Garden, lighting by Images by Lighting.

views

Every day in the event world is a chance to try something new. A host's interests or lifestyle may inspire a concept, and then it's up to me to draw on all my creative resources and experience and turn it into a full-fledged vision. Nothing stretches your imagination like fashioning an environment from nothing.

Oh, How Charming!

Lisa Vorce

How does a woman go from working in corporate technology to traveling the world and planning exotic, unforgettable events? With style, of course. When Lisa Vorce found herself disheartened to be sitting behind a desk all day, the UC Berkley graduate realized it was time to follow what made her happy. Before long she discovered boutique event planning, a career that requires sociability, travel, creativity, and hard work. With her goal fully realized, Lisa opened Oh, How Charming! in 2001.

Hosts looking to throw a well-produced but understated event while receiving concierge-style attention often find themselves drawn to Lisa. Enthusiastic and deeply in love with what she does, her genuine personality is reflected in the care she shows her hosts. It's not uncommon for her to talk every day with them, nor is it unusual for her to do everything within her power to make a host and every single one of their guests happy.

While Lisa does take advantage of the amazing resources Southern California has to offer, she specializes in destination events. Whether she's in Mexico or France, partnering with local artisans and truly discovering the flavor and history of a locale is vital. This opportunity to work with different cultures and personalities inspires Lisa's event concepts, with fabrics, jewelry, art, china patterns, or architecture often serving as muses. Because of this, her events radiate individual personality and have an extremely fluid and styled sensibility.

The bride loved antique chandeliers, and had been collecting them for years to use at her wedding. They became the focal point of the vintage, flea market-inspired design, which included a fresh color palette and eclectic clusters of mercury glass.

Photograph by Thayer Allyson Gowdy

Photograph by Elizabeth Messina

Photograph by Elizabeth Messina

Photograph by Elizabeth Messina

Above: Hand-rolled cigars and a tequila bar are just two ways we incorporated local Mexican flair into a beach wedding.

Right: Some hosts are exploring alternatives to using fresh florals, which in some of the warmer climates is actually a very smart decision. The rattan balls lining the aisle have a playful quality which reminded me of beach balls—very fitting for the setting.

Facing page: For each destination event, I typically visit the location for a week early on by myself to explore local markets and source as much as I can. Local artisans crafted the stars, rattan discs, tables, and chairs for the wedding. I've acquired so many incredible pieces of furniture and décor that I keep a warehouse in Mexico from which local resorts now rent out my treasures.

Photograph by Elizabeth Messina

Photograph by Elizabeth Messina

"I love being the last person the bride talks to before she walks down the aisle."

—Lisa Vorce

Left: The intense beauty of a private estate in Costa Careyes, Mexico was enhanced with hundreds of wax cylinders cradling votive candles.

Facing page: Silk chiffon and raw linen combined airy sweetness with an earthy sensibility. The heart-shaped candelabras were a find in an antique shop in Puerto Vallarta, and the menu, printed on bark paper, surprised guests with traditional artwork when they flipped it over.

Photograph by Elizabeth Messina

Photograph by Elizabeth Messina

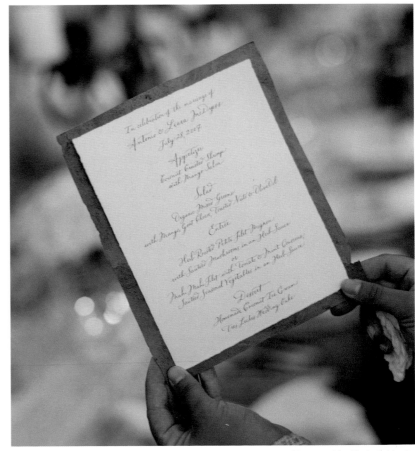

Photograph by Elizabeth Messina

Photograph by Aaron Delesie

Photograph by Aaron Delesie

Above and right: It would make absolutely no sense to cart boxes of décor to a foreign country where such a dazzling abundance—both manmade and natural—already exists.

Facing page: A combination of ruffles, fabric flowers, and romantic touches went into the sweetheart table for a couple that had eloped to Mexico.

Photograph by Aaron Delesie

Photograph by Aaron Delesie

Photograph by Aaron Delesie

Above: Some of the locations we use for events aren't famous in a widespread sense, but they do possess a history and culture that are very special. We always try to respect the authenticity of the space, but at the same time heighten the drama and personalize the surroundings for the host. A centuries-old niche that normally houses a statue of the Virgin Mary, or an altar traditionally used to display portraits of loved ones during Day of the Dead celebrations, provide unique and meaningful backdrops for a cake or a sweets table.

Facing page: We work very hard to blend our designs into a location's natural surroundings. Using grapevine accented with potted lavender and olive trees, we created a U-shaped loggia from which to suspend a collection of French wire chandeliers. Partnering with local French companies produced fresh cherries and champagne to be enjoyed by the guests.

Photograph by Elizabeth Messina

Photograph by Elizabeth Messina

Photograph by Elizabeth Messina

Photograph by Aaron Delesie

Photograph by Aaron Delesie

"To produce a truly extraordinary event, you have to understand who your hosts are at their core."

—Lisa Vorce

An intimate wedding in the Bahamas was built on lush scenery and an enchanting table setting.

views

A destination event is exotic and thrilling, but it also comes with its fair share of extra baggage. Keep in mind that the added expense often required may limit some guests from attending, and others may not fare so well with a long journey. However, it's nearly impossible to duplicate that exhilarating feeling travel inspires, and gathering friends and loved ones together in a far-flung place can create memories of more than just the special event.

EXQUISITE EVENTS
NIKKI KHAN

Celebrations are often steeped in tradition, with cultural or religious instructions shaping the décor, wardrobe, and even cuisine. When dealing with Indian and Pakistani festivities, however, an intricate understanding of the culture's nuances and sensitivities is even more crucial. Few event planners have the necessary background to successfully carry off such an event, but Nikki Khan is more than qualified. Born in Pakistan, Nikki spent her formative years in Switzerland attending an elite finishing school. She found designing tables and arranging flowers so appealing that even after beginning a career as a clinical dietician in California, Nikki decided to follow her passion and work in special events.

Exquisite Events, formed in 2001, specializes in the type of elaborate, multi-day events that the Indian and Pakistani cultures are known for. Most of these parties require at least a year of planning, if not more, and utilize every resource and spare ounce of energy Nikki possesses. To ensure that the incredible attention to detail and level of personal attention never flags, Nikki and her team produce only 12 events a year. But when you figure that each event encompasses roughly four separate parties, the true number climbs much higher.

To help hotels and other organizations better understand these types of events, Nikki has joined the lecture circuit to share her insights and experiences all across the nation. Educating venues and vendors from a first-hand point of view helps elucidate the most important concept: tradition is the lifeblood of culture.

Seven back-to-back events afford the opportunity to create different designs based on the purpose and significance of each gathering. The keywords the bride came up with for her ceremony and large sit-down dinner reception were romance, intimacy, and English garden. The sumptuous tent was converted from ceremony to reception while the guests enjoyed cocktails in an adjoining tent.

Photograph by John Solano Photography

Photograph by John Solano Photography

Photograph by John Solano Photography

Photograph by John Solano Photography

Photograph by John Solano Photography

Photograph by John Solano Photography

Before we even get to the wedding itself, prayers are held at the bride's home before the bride and groom's parents each host a Sangeet. A Sangeet serves as the official kick-off for all the revelry about to come, with music, dancing, and fun lasting into the wee hours. A henna party follows the Sangeet, then the ornate ceremony and reception take place, and it all concludes with the sophisticated grand reception.

"All of the long hours and hard work are so worth it when you finally get to see the host's reaction."

—Nikki Khan

Photograph by Andrena Photography

Photograph by Andrena Photography

Photograph by John Solano Photography

Photograph by John Solano Photography

Above and right: I've never seen so many people enter a reception and marvel in awe in the way they did for my enchanted forest design. Birds chirped from cages dripping with flowers, lanterns and votives hung from live trees, and each table was named for a famous couple from classic Eastern or Western love stories. The newlyweds' sweetheart table, of course, bore their names.

Facing page: A bride's infatuation with Paris and all things French allowed me to bring in ruffles and feathers, creating a grand reception that brought to mind can-can dancers and glamorous bistros. Pink and amber lights glinted off the glossy, custom-made mahogany dance floor, ropes of pearls hung from the stunning centerpieces, and special thought was given to the napkin fold, done in the form of a rose. The men received vintage wine bottles as favors, while the ladies were presented with silver dishes crafted in India.

Photograph by John Solano Photography

Photograph by John Solano Photography

Traditional practices abound in a Sikh wedding, such as the ceremony always having to end before noon. Other important elements include clearing all furniture for the ceremony—since traditionally guests sit on the floor—and not allowing meat dishes or alcohol to be served until the ceremony is concluded and the Holy Book removed from the premises. Though once that happens, the corks get popped and the party really starts!

Photograph by John Solano Photography

Photograph by John Solano Photography

Photograph by John Solano Photography

Photograph by John Solano Photography

Photograph by John Solano Photography

Photograph by John Solano Photography

Photograph by John Solano Photography

"Hosts should arrive at their own event as guests, relaxed and ready to enjoy the celebration."

—Nikki Khan

Right: The bride wanted to use the same structure employed at her Sikh and Hindu ceremonies for her sweetheart table at the luncheon. The whole room was awash in a pink and amber glow, and beautiful centerpieces of twigs were created with fuchsias, oranges, and a hint of coral.

Facing page top: Some very important elements of a successful henna event include marigolds, the colors green and yellow, and female guests dancing and singing traditional songs. Touches of fuchsia give the space an added vibrancy. While the sunken center of the room had only low furniture and a collection of brightly colored pillows, a stage was erected to hold the bride, groom, and their families while they received their decoration.

Facing page bottom: I built a Sangeet entirely around the concept of peacock feathers. The iridescent cobalt blue, turquoise, emerald green, and bronze provided a lovely starting point for a room that eventually included swirling light projections and flower arrangements studded with the feathers. A swing imported from India resided underneath a canopy built from twigs and hung with lanterns.

Photograph by Andrena Photography

views

Creating multi-day Indian events can be challenging and requires tremendous amounts of planning, knowledge, and hard work. Since each event has a distinct personality of its own and no two events are alike, keen vision, creativity, and unparalleled attention to detail are required. I am lucky to have a team that is dedicated, hard working, and understands the nuances and sensitivities of Indian culture.

DETAILS DETAILS, WEDDING AND EVENT PLANNING

JEANNIE SAVAGE

While putting together her own Santa Barbara wedding, Jeannie Savage realized her passion for event planning. After 10 years in the hospitality industry and working as a general manager at several full-service hotels, this discovery didn't exactly come as a surprise, but it did motivate Jeannie to start Details Details. After working solo for nearly three years, Jeannie assembled the talented group of hospitality professionals that currently round out the Details Details team. Now her company plans one-of-a-kind weddings and special events that benefit from Jeannie's animated personality, impeccable style, and razor-sharp attention to—you guessed it—details.

Joannie and her team work early on to establish a high level of trust between themselves and their event hosts, many of whom require the utmost in privacy, security, and dedication. This, combined with a sunny and confident attitude, goes a long way toward putting beleaguered and frantic minds at ease. As Jeannie points out, it's practically impossible to have a good time when the party planner is stressed. Fortunately, the combined years of service experience, industry knowledge, and absolute passion guarantee that any event planned by Details Details will be carried out with uncompromising excellence and energy.

From the first meeting to the final guest's departure, nothing is overlooked. With services ranging from basic guidance to day-of assistance to all-inclusive production, Details Details offers a wide range of levels designed to suit all needs.

By constructing multiple white canopies on a cliffside lawn, Fiori Fresco Special Events achieved a cool seaside elegance while enhancing the already dazzling view of the Pacific Ocean. Simple white hydrangea arrangements, natural wood boxes filled with sand, and subtle hints of aqua and starfish all enriched the decor. The clever use of capiz chandeliers amplified the salty sea breeze and rhythmic crashing of the surf.

Photograph by Joe Photo

Photograph by Barber Photography

"An event planner's priority should be to understand every host's taste and individual style, and work with them until everything is exactly as they had envisioned."

—Jeannie Savage

Photograph by Victor Sizemore Photography

Photograph by Barnet Photography

Above: It's wonderful when someone knows what they like, but it often takes a designer's eye to combine favorites to the best advantage. Too much of one color or flower can be monochromatic, so using varying shades and textures provides more visual interest. The abundance of orchids and the color purple could have been overwhelming if not for White Lilac's subtle blending of the two with more unexpected elements.

Right: I'm finding that grooms are becoming more involved in their wedding plans, challenging the designers to appeal to a more masculine sensibility while still providing all the feminine touches that a bride typically dreams of. White Lilac's careful use of pewter and silver with lots of mirrored and soft floral accents kept this design from being too harsh or cold.

Facing page top: To create the effect of Old World charm with a hint of modern design, Fiori Fresco Special Events created banquet seating vignettes with custom camel suede banquettes, elegant table runners, and rustic tabletop lamps. The remaining communal tables featured distressed wood tops decorated with rusted wrought-iron obelisks and faux stone garden ornamentation, all embellished with flowers and studded with moss and flower balls.

Facing page bottom: When the request is to convert a typical, non-descript ballroom into a 1940s jazz supper club using only a color palette of black, white, and red, you know there is a challenge involved. Together with Fiori Fresco Special Events, we achieved the swanky and glamorous supper club feel by building terraces with gold Art Deco-inspired railings. Décor was kept simple yet elegant, allowing the understatement to make the statement. A 27-piece orchestra specializing in '40s and '50s jazz and performers singing the melodies of Frank Sinatra and Ella Fitzgerald added the perfect finishing touch.

Photograph by Hoffmann Photography

Photograph by Ira Lippke Studios

Photograph by Jessica Claire

"The harder you work before an event, the more you can focus on what really matters on the day: seeing the joy on everyone's faces."

—Jeannie Savage

Photograph by Victor Sizemore Photography

Photograph by Ira Lippke Studios

Photograph by Ira Lippke Studios

It sounds cliché, but every event really is different and should be treated as such. Sometimes a couple might want to incorporate their love of travel and collection of Asian antiques into their function. Another person might want to evoke a cozy, comfortable atmosphere by introducing couches and floor lamps, as if the guests had been invited into their hosts' home to celebrate. One event we did featured an ice cream sundae bar, a whimsical take on the conventional wedding cake. Whatever the reason or whoever the host, it's important to feature as much personality as possible.

views

I want guests to be wowed the moment they enter the ballroom, and again when they start looking at all the details. So as a room is being decorated, I always step in and out a few times throughout the process. That way I get the same first impression that the guests will when they enter. The gradual addition of lighting, flowers, table settings—each brings another level of drama. When the room takes my breath away, it's done.

KRISTIN BANTA EVENTS
KRISTIN BANTA

When looking for the perfect event planner, some basic assets are a necessity: creativity, warmth, knowledge, experience, attention to detail, and passion about event design. But how about trained in welding? Apprenticed in interior design? Experienced in catering, florals, stage lighting, and carpentry? Kristin Banta possesses all of these credentials and more, having worked in every facet involved with event production and design. It's these unusual skills that make Kristin so versatile, accomplished, respected by her peers and beloved by her exclusive clientele.

In order to provide the utmost in personalized attention, Kristin accepts only 10-12 events a year where she does full event production and design. There are many event planners in Southern California, and all differ in style and approach, but since she is also a designer, Kristin uses her unique knowledge to develop a full planning experience where she can dig deep to figure out who her clients are and bring their visions to life in grand scale.

Kristin started out designing window displays and events for a fashion designer. That experience segued into planning events for non-profit organizations as well as recording artists, and later to the production side of a major record label. It was from there, in 2000, that she established her own company, Kristin Banta Events. Now her events, much like her career, benefit from her willingness to push the envelope, inspiring the exciting question, "What's she going to do next?"

Working with artistic people such as actors and musicians always allows for the opportunity to take creative risks. In my attempt to create a gypsy tent village for a recording artist, I sought out a variety of fabrics with unfinished seams, which were layered, bustled, and thrown over the tables in an eclectic Bohemian vibe. Objects like compasses, urns, and chunky glassware were landscaped on top of the tables, to look like treasures collected by explorers while sailing around the globe. I wanted each element to feel as though it had a different origin, conveying warmth and romance while still being cohesive.

Photograph by Miki & Sonja Photography

Photograph by Miki & Sonja Photography

Photograph by Miki & Sonja Photography

Photograph by Miki & Sonja Photography

Photograph by Victor Sizemore Photography

Above: The graphic ultrasuede table runner adorning the mirrored tabletop provided inspiration with its vibrant raspberry color and masculine sensibility. To offset the strength of the print and soften the look, we used small but lush flower arrangements and a variety of curvaceous vessels of varied heights. I couldn't find suitable napkin rings, so at the last minute I wrapped each napkin with reflective silver wire to add texture and originality.

Facing page: The wedding of Good Charlotte guitarist Billy Martin and Linzi Williamson remains one of my favorites, partly because they had such dramatic personal style. The event had a haunted quality to it, as if it were happening in a romantic, ancient European village. We didn't use many florals, but instead covered the two long tables with vintage pieces and Victorian collectables. The success of any event depends upon the stimulation of multiple senses, thus each guest had a different table setting, which provided a visual impact.

"If we oversimplify the plan, we take the soul out of the spectacle. Dare to design from within."

—Kristin Banta

Photograph by elizabeth messina, kissthegroom.com

Above and left: Something I truly love to do is to bring nature to indoor spaces and make the outdoors feel more intimate. I wanted to transform a ballroom to be reminiscent of a Mediterranean piazza, so I had pepper trees and olive trees placed throughout the room. We hung Tivoli lights in the corners and created a custom stage front covered in creeping fig to make it look like an authentic element of the piazza. An aged stone fountain with floating blossoms was placed in the center of the room, and all the florals looked as though they could have been picked from a hillside near the villa. Raw wooden tables and various natural fibers created a feeling of European hospitality.

Facing page: The cobblestones of Two Rodeo, a street in the heart of Beverly Hills, inspired me to reproduce a French street scene to appear as if the local merchants and villagers had all contributed wares from their shops and attics for a village feast. In the midst of some of the world's most revered brands, I thought it would be fun to showcase items that seemed as though they had been abandoned for ages and then rediscovered and put on display. It was a nine-course dinner, providing the guests ample time to examine the collection and speculate over its rich and colorful history.

Photograph by elizabeth messina, kissthegroom.com

"Take risks! Use unexpected elements, find your own voice, and definitely have fun."

—Kristin Banta

Photograph by Evoke Photography

Photograph by Evoke Photography

Photograph by Miki & Sonja Photography

Photograph by Kerry Corcoran, David Michael Photography

Photograph by Jennifer Roper Photography

"The challenge of any event is to make it original yet relevant to the host; the uniqueness of each individual is what inspires me."

—Kristin Banta

Right: There are three things I think every design can benefit from: texture, dimension, and personality. At the end of the day, your event should reflect who you are and what you love.

Facing page top: A quick way to add visual interest is to play with the design of the linens. Some tables might have only a runner, while others can be swathed in copious amounts of fabric. The key to making the look harmonious is having each tabletop tell a similar story with its décor.

Facing page bottom left: One groom, who could only see in shades of gray, inspired me to create a wedding that conveyed a significant visual impact that would not be dependent upon one's ability to see color. For the ceremony, we covered the white Hotel Bel Air gazebo in hundreds of monochromatic burgundy red florals, emphasizing texture and dimension. Following the ceremony, the guests were escorted into a cocktail area, a transitional space decorated entirely in champagne hues, intended to be a visual palate cleanser. The ballroom was completely enveloped with multiple fabrics and décor in a color spectrum of pearl, silver, platinum, charcoal, and pale gray. By using varied hues of the same color we created one of our most dramatic weddings to date.

Facing page bottom right: Celebrating inside an old car showroom allowed for the mingling of both modern and organic textures. Cement floors, hanging glass lanterns, reclaimed wooden tables and chairs, nubby Russian linen tablecloths, not to mention unexpected flower pairings all combined to form a quirky yet splendid atmosphere.

Photograph by Evoke Photography

views

It's easy from a production standpoint to be formulaic, to make every table setting the same. But by mixing things up—playing with different textures, colors, and design elements—you will ensure that your guests are stimulated by the visual aspects of the space in addition to the food, wine, entertainment, and company. As the discoveries unfold, your guests will have a lasting impression they will talk about long after the event is over.

LEVINE FOX EVENTS, INC.

DIANE LEVINE | ALYSON FOX

Some of the best partnerships grow out of years of working together, but few can top the relationship shared by Diane Levine and Alyson Fox. Widely regarded as taste-making, organizational divas, they have designed and coordinated weddings, theme parties, birthday celebrations, and baby showers for many of Hollywood's A-list and other lucky hosts. The reason for their effortless rapport and confident collaboration is simple: they're mother and daughter.

Diane's background in interior design and later event production made it nearly impossible for Alyson not to inherit a knack for design. Since forming their own company in 1997, Diane and Alyson have worked diligently to achieve a well-deserved reputation for creativity, attention to detail, and professionalism. Each has discovered her own niche, with Diane constantly tweaking the old and reinventing the standard for sophistication, and Alyson keeping a pulse on the ever-changing event scene. The result is a boutique company that lavishes attention on its hosts while simultaneously focusing on their individual tastes, priorities, and desires.

However, Levine Fox Events doesn't stop with its design. Creativity is what challenges them, and the company's versatility is limitless—menu and music selection, entertainment procurement, and introductions to outstanding vendors are just part of the package these ladies provide. Over the years they have developed terrific relationships with their vendors, understanding the importance of having a solid team to work with. And few are better qualified to appreciate a solid team than Diane Levine and Alyson Fox.

An outdated ballroom becomes instantly more stylish with the construction of open-sided canopies. The tapestry fabric in deep shades of brown, with its Old World elegance, creates a sophisticated ambience. That pattern repeats throughout the room, in valances, runners, napkin cuffs, even the lighting design projected on the dance floor. Two Venetian chandeliers add a warm romantic glow to the head table vignette.

Photograph by Joe Buissink

Photograph by John Solano Photography

Photograph by John Solano Photography

Photograph by John Solano Photography

More and more people are embracing the concept of a dual party design. For example, the ceremony might be done in shades of antique white and champagne, with clean lines and minimal embellishment. But when guests enter the reception area, dramatic colors and more intricate décor reveal a spicier side of the couple. A wedding at The Beverly Hills Hotel used this idea to great effect: roses in a lattice pattern served as a backdrop for the unity candle table and hand-calligraphied escort cards carried a delicate filigree pattern. The reception, however, was done as a "Latin Tango Club," with black lace accents, deep red draping, and a glossy black dance floor emblazoned with the couple's initials.

"Anticipating ahead of time all the details necessary to make a smooth event happen exemplifies great service."

—Alyson Fox

Photograph by John Solano Photography

Above and left: One of the main design elements of the tent allowed guests to enjoy a spectacular outdoor setting in addition to the beautiful tableau created inside. Keeping the sides of the draped tent open let guests bask in the surrounding greenery and later enjoy the atmospheric landscape lighting. Just outside the large canopied dinner tent, silk dupioni umbrellas were positioned over the hightop cocktail tables. Shades of whites and creams, together with touches of neutral taupe, added a refreshing coolness to the hot afternoon sun.

Facing page top: No detail is too small. Each décor element in the place setting design is there to specifically reflect the formality and elegance of the overall ambience.

Facing page bottom: Adding a surprise disco-themed afterparty ensures your guests will definitely not leave before the cake is cut. We brought in sleek, modern furniture and draped the walls in black silk, providing a great contrast for the graphic printed screen, the design of which was replicated on the cake. Shadow boxes for professional dancers and white padded booths for the DJ and two bars turned the room into a hot, hip nightclub.

Photograph by John Solano Photography

"Each event is unique in its own statement."

—Diane Levine

Photograph by John Solano Photography

Photograph by John Solano Photography

Photograph by John Solano Photography

"Time and energy are imperative to satisfy a host's needs."

—Diane Levine

Right: Minimalistic in design, the two pool floats complemented the other floral accents placed throughout the party and brought visual interest to the large pool. Bamboo accents, positioned along the bottom of the dark wood float, correlated with the sushi station and large architectural floral structure in the center of the lounge area. Simplistic touches of greenery along with large pillar candles surrounded by hurricane glass produced a glow throughout the evening.

Facing page: The hosts wished to impart a casual and upbeat lounge atmosphere, and we achieved that by creating a comfortable club environment, with seating that allowed guests to enjoy the evening's food and festivities without the formality of table service. Streamlined sofa and ottoman groupings in white with black accents were positioned within tailored, open-sided canopies, the valances of which were accented with an updated Greek key motif. The glow from black Venetian glass chandeliers under each canopy, along with soft ambient lighting, added drama to the scene.

Photograph by John Solano Photography

views

We tend to work with our hosts more than once, so we try extra hard to never duplicate a design we've done before. The same pool of guests might be attending the engagement party, bridal shower, wedding, baby shower, and various birthday parties over the years, and it's up to us to present them with something fresh and exciting each time. Since the creativity in event design is endless, we truly enjoy the constant search for new ideas.

EMILY SMILEY FINE WEDDINGS & SOIRÉES

EMILY SMILEY

An expert at translating people's ideas and requests into a comprehensive vision, event planner Emily Smiley has established a reputation in the industry for her ability to execute plans to perfection. Her friendly yet professional demeanor makes her equal parts best friend, confidant, and trusted expert for all things creative.

Emily brings years of experience in hospitality, incredible organizational skills, and a wealth of knowledge about the event industry to every soireé she plans. Her mother has been involved in the floral, catering, and hotel business for over 30 years, and it was her expertise and encouragement that influenced Emily to learn all the necessary ingredients for fashioning the perfect celebration. Since establishing her namesake firm in 2004, she has placed an emphasis on integrity and creativity, instilling trust in her hosts by ensuring that every detail, no matter how small, will be attended.

As much as she delights in sharing in the momentous occasions swirling around her, Emily firmly maintains that her duty is to make sure things go off without a hitch. While hosts can easily become overwhelmed by the many emotions, people, and details that surround a big event, Emily has learned what an immense help it is to have someone manage all the elements so the host can truly revel in the moment without a worry. Even when a key contributor may want to take the reins, Emily is always ready to explain and defend, with a smile of course, the actualization of the host's vision for the event.

My siblings work with me, and our close family trust really gives me the confidence to know that anything my company promises will be delivered at the highest quality.

Photograph by Darin Fong

I love events that are fashion forward, innovative, and fresh. The color, texture, and shimmer of repeated tablescapes make a powerful design statement.

"The ultimate peace of mind is knowing that all the details have been attended to before the event even begins."

—Emily Smiley

Photograph by Darin Fong

Photograph by Suzanne Hansen

Photograph by Darin Fong

Photograph by Tim Otto

Photograph by Lauren Ong

Photograph by Boyd Harris

"Maintaining good relationships with vendors produces a flawless event."

—Emily Smiley

Whether you're taking advantage of Southern California's perfect climate and delicious views or creating your own wonderland within a ballroom, the event is really about showcasing your own personal aesthetic. That level of taste can carry through to all of the details, from hors d'oeuvres to florals to the attire and jewelry.

views

Before really diving into planning any big event, you should take a moment to sit down and figure out what is most important to you. What do you want your guests to experience and remember? Whether it's a wedding or a social event, your planner should work to ensure the atmosphere and memories you want your guests to cherish. The day should reflect who you are, not who your designers are. The event planner's job is to make your dream event a reality.

GELLER EVENTS
DEBBIE GELLER

Some say ignorance is bliss, but Debbie Geller believes that the more knowledge she can attain, the better off she— and the event hosts who retain her—will be. With her first degree in English literature, she has since studied graphic design, been trained as a chef, and spent nearly two decades learning and perfecting the ins and outs of celebrations.

Born out of Debbie's love for the unusual, Geller Events has embraced the idea of going off the beaten path. To ensure each event receives the attention it deserves, Debbie limits the number of projects they take on. This select nature has served the team well. From designing events for renowned comedians and well-known celebrities to creating the look for several television weddings, including a green wedding for "Days of Our Lives," Debbie has done it all.

The relationship with the event host, which is often cultivated over the years through several celebrations, is the core of the process. Taking advantage of her numerous skill sets, Debbie presents a sketch of her design ideas after listening carefully to the host's desires and goals for the party. With inspiration arriving from virtually any avenue—from fashion and magazines to traveling and restaurants—Debbie and her team then forge into new territory to establish a festivity that ultimately radiates the host's personality and goals.

Each event has its own exciting challenges, and a reception at Vibiana, a former cathedral turned event venue, was no exception. To accommodate the grand scale of the space while remaining in the host's budget, we created centerpieces of varying heights, some as tall as six feet. Warm, soft lighting enveloped the space, creating an intimacy that can often be lost with dramatic high ceilings.

Photograph by Stephanie Hogue

Photograph by Jay Lawrence Goldman

Above and left: A birthday party was designed to replicate an English men's social club where the guest of honor had spent his youth. To impart a cozy atmosphere, we draped the ceiling and paneled the walls. The birthday honoree is well-known for being a pillar of society, so we designed the space—which is all inside a tent—to feel permanent and important, without going over the top.

Facing page: A James Bond-themed birthday celebration was designed with a male audience in mind. There were Bond gadgets to play with and sets that brought out the child in every guest. A rocket "lifted off" and filled the room with smoke to signify the end of the cocktail hour, and guests were ushered into the main room through doors designed as bank vault doors.

Photograph by Jay Lawrence Goldman

"A successful event occurs when guests walk in and immediately see the reflection of the host in the atmosphere."

—Debbie Geller

Photograph by Jay Lawrence Goldman

Photograph by Jay Lawrence Goldman

Photograph by Joe Buissink

Photograph by Joe Buissink

Photograph by Joe Buissink

Photograph by Brian Kramer

"Find something that inspires you and translate it into a room."
—Debbie Geller

Right: In the Bahamas, creating elegance in a tropical environment was our focus. In the reception tent, a stagefront made entirely of seashells, tablecloths accented with pearls, and additional shells in the flowers created the canvas for a black-tie island wedding. For the afterparty on the beach, we enhanced the natural setting with dramatic lighting for a lively feel.

Facing page: Inspired by Art Nouveau design, the bride brought us a poster that exuded the feel she was looking for. We transformed the image and had it painted on glass, which was featured at the wedding as the cornerstone of the design. It served as the inspiration for the event and drove everything from the colors to the texture of the draping and use of vintage elements. The vibrant, fun ambience perfectly reflected the host's personality.

Photograph by Brian Kramer

views

Instead of letting the flowers tell the entire story, first create an incredible environment. Then, accent with the flowers in key locations to enhance the space without overwhelming it. This allows the eye to rest on beautiful focal points.

INTERNATIONAL EVENT COMPANY

JONATHAN REEVES

"It was the best day of my life!" is the greatest compliment Jonathan Reeves can receive, and he makes it his goal to hear it at every event he plans. In 2000, Jonathan entered private event planning, drawing upon his experience as the director of catering at The Beverly Hills Hotel and the Four Seasons Los Angeles. Seven years later he opened International Event Company, and his events quickly became known for how they capture the excitement of entertaining.

Each event is considered an opportunity to fulfill a host's dreams and make them a reality. When hired to create once-in-a-lifetime celebrations, Jonathan sets frazzled minds at ease by reminding them that he and his dedicated team at IEC are there to make sure what is promised is delivered. It's also reassuring to know that Jonathan and event coordinators Margot Hummel, Mari Tsuchiyama, and Cora Kaplan have years of professional experience deftly handling every sort of event imaginable. Noticing that Los Angeleans are especially adept at putting a personal stamp on their festivities, Jonathan is always enthused to share his own knowledge, gained from years of contributing to a kaleidoscope of parties.

The collaborative atmosphere at IEC is instantly apparent. Besides inviting hosts to share their wishes and ideas for the event, constant communication ensures that everyone is on the same page. After assembling a team of proven vendors who are committed to the success of the event, Jonathan encourages his hosts to focus on their guests and entrust the planning details to IEC. Making sure everything goes off without a hitch is, after all, their specialty.

Recreating a 1940s nightclub with sleek Art Deco influences gave the guests carte blanche to dress to the nines. Women floated about the room wearing spectacular gowns while the men donned dapper white dinner jackets.

Photograph by Nadine Froger Photography

Photograph by Nadine Froger Photography

Photograph by Nadine Froger Photography

Photograph by Nadine Froger Photography

Photograph by John Russo

Photograph by John Russo

Photograph by Nadine Froger Photography

Photograph by Nadine Froger Photography

Photograph by Jay Lawrence Goldman

"A seasoned event planner is your 'insurance' to guarantee a magnificent celebration."

—Jonathan Reeves

Taking a raw space and converting it into another world is one of my favorite challenges. The day of setup we run the show with what we call "organized excitement," relying on detailed timelines and a positive attitude to fit all the pieces of the puzzle together.

Photograph by Yitzhak Dalal

views

Choose to work with someone you connect with, someone you really trust. You should be able to enjoy the process of planning an event by leaving the details to them. By sharing as much information as possible, you will be free to think about other things—like what you're going to wear!

MINDY WEISS PARTY CONSULTANTS
MINDY WEISS

The New York Times called her "one of the top five wedding planners in the United States." Her client list reads like a who's who of Hollywood royalty. She not only runs her own business and exclusive gift product line, but has also written a 400-page book chock-full of tips, information, and advice about throwing the perfect event. But Mindy Weiss is surprisingly relatable, a woman who's devoted to her hosts and passionate about her profession.

With roots in the invitation business, Mindy never really saw event planning as a tantalizing option given the staggering level of commitment—and impact on personal time—it requires. But Mindy's mother was a seasoned hostess, throwing fabulous parties and instilling in Mindy what it took to plan a memorable soireé. With event planning in her blood, Mindy started her own business in 1992, and since then, her accolades have only mounted.

Now known as the woman who orchestrated Heidi Klum and Seal's wedding, along with parties, showers, and other celebrations for countless boldfaced names, Mindy doesn't let her status get in the way of her perfectionist planning. Hosts come to her for a relaxed, one-on-one approach, a method that guarantees their event will not be a factory experience. Nearly all of the time, Mindy and her hosts forge a lifelong friendship, working together on each happy occasion that comes next.

A big square table makes a bold statement, but it can be difficult to fill. By swathing it with roses and greenery, the table became an art piece, one that provided different angles with each descending step the guests took.

Photograph by Yitzhak Dalal

Photograph by Simone and Martin Photography

Above and left: A Moulin Rouge-themed birthday party opened up a whole realm of fun possibilities. Since the guest list was small and the ballroom large, oversized props and furniture helped balance out the scale. Provocative touches, like flouncy, corseted chair covers resembling a can-can dancer's dress, enhanced the flirty vibe.

Facing page: Even if you want to display different sides of your personality throughout the course of your event, a sense of cohesion keeps guests from feeling overwhelmed. Roses and elegant chandeliers united the inside and outside of the reception tent, and more roses were used to delineate three separate ceremony aisles: two for guests and one reserved solely for the bride.

Photograph by Simone and Martin Photography

Photograph by Simone and Martin Photography

Photograph by Simone and Martin Photography

Photograph by Simone and Martin Photography

Photograph by Simone and Martin Photography

Photograph by Simone and Martin Photography

Photograph by Simone and Martin Photography

Photograph by Simone and Martin Photography

Photograph by John Solano Photography

"Think of the possibilities, not the problems."

—Mindy Weiss

Top: A 50th birthday party for a very distinguished man meant banishing anything frilly or frou-frou. Modern, tailored lines, a palette of taupe and navy, and large screens providing a better view of surprise guest performer Stevie Wonder all fit the bill.

Bottom: In order to take full advantage of the oceanfront location, we constructed a tent with a real wooden deck—complete with patio furniture—so guests could truly enjoy the Malibu sunset.

Facing page: Going from breezy cocktails overlooking the water to a sophisticated mod lounge, then juxtaposing an elegant dinner with a surprise disco meant guests were amazed at every turn.

Photograph by Simone and Martin Photography

views

I've worked in some absolutely beautiful locations and with many wonderful vendors, but just when I think I know it all, a host will suggest a person, place, or item I hadn't even thought about. Don't be afraid to voice your opinions to your planner—they may lead to something spectacular.

Yifat Oren & Associates
YIFAT OREN

If you can't immediately tell who designed the glorious party you're attending, Yifat Oren considers that a good thing. A designer revered for her elegant and unfussy style, Yifat runs her business with the belief that each event should shine on its own, never drawing comparisons to other soirées or relying on a celebrity signature.

For even though Yifat is something of a celebrity in her own right, having designed high-profile events around the globe for stylish hosts and Hollywood's elite for more than a decade, she would never dream of letting her status eclipse an event. Instead, hosts are drawn to her notion of "couture events," where every detail is custom-designed to suit their personality and vision. Rather than follow trends, Yifat and her team at Yifat Oren & Associates create them, inspiring concepts that quickly influence others on the event scene.

No matter how many elements are involved, a party designed by Yifat Oren never seems overproduced. There may be hundreds of tiny details, complex travel plans, and scores of people to contend with, but the overall outcome is always seamless, effortless. Yifat was drawn to her profession because it combines all the things she loves—design, art, great food, and travel—but it is the opportunity to see beauty in everything, and creating beauty for hosts and guests alike, that truly captivates her.

Unexpected touches put a modern twist on a classic English garden. Silver candelabras, vintage vessels, and romantic pastel floral arrangements set the tone of a bygone era. The placement of privet hedges, English lavender, statuary, and moss-filled urns in the table centers furthers the fairytale-like atmosphere.

Photograph by Dana Hargitay

Photograph by Lara Porzak

Above: Soft, flowing organza and dozens of custom-made feather lanterns turn a standard tent into a whimsical scene, complete with artfully placed butterflies and dragonflies on menus and in the centerpieces.

Left: A 200-year-old working coffee plantation in Montego Bay, Jamaica provided an ideal setting for an outdoor rehearsal dinner. Mismatched wooden chairs, locally inspired centerpieces, woven baskets piled full of plantains, and strings of floating lights made it a flavorful party by the Caribbean Sea.

Facing page: Instead of standing under a traditional huppah in front of their guests, the couple was encircled by family and friends under a suspended huppah of nature-inspired flowers in rich, deep colors. The raised mound constructed of moss and twigs designated where they would become husband and wife, creating a design element both above and below the couple. Custom-made wooden tables were adorned with Manzanita branches, grapevines, and lush florals, creating delicate trellises under which the guests dined.

Photograph by Lara Porzak

Photograph by Gia Canali

Photograph by Gia Canali

Photograph by Gia Canali

Photograph by Benjamin Norman

Photograph by Benjamin Norman

Photograph by Benjamin Norman

Photograph by Lara Porzak

"A great collaboration often yields impeccable results."

—Yifat Oren

Right: Spectacular fireworks overlooking Montego Bay were a climactic and dramatic ending to a magnificent night.

Facing page: For a party with an updated Moroccan casbah theme, custom fabric printed in India lined the interior of the lounge tent. Editing out flowers in favor of metallic and glass accessories and oversized tropical leaves projected a clean yet ornate effect. As the night wore on, hundreds of delicately lit lanterns immersed in the water created a luminous backdrop for the celebration on the dock.

views

We as event designers need to be very pliable. It's not our vision we're bringing to life, it's yours: your vision through our eyes. Only through constructive collaboration can we help you decide what inspires you and come up with that perfect aesthetic.

BEST EVENTS

JEFFREY BEST

If you ask Jeffrey Best how he came to be the owner of seven restaurants and his own event planning firm, he'll tell you it's because he was a good dishwasher. While working nearly every restaurant job over a span of 15 years, Jeffrey took notice of what people enjoyed while dining, how a room should look to make them feel comfortable, and the most effective ways to present food. He filed that information away until it was time to open his own successful restaurants, and when his patrons started asking him to deliver a lunch here, cater a business meeting there, and then provide food and decoration for their parties, Jeffrey realized perhaps he should dive into the event business.

Still firmly ensconced in both worlds, Jeffrey somehow finds time not only to plan events, but to plan the kind of events that send ripples through the celebrity and corporate worlds. His ability to deliver a theatrical experience marked by spectacular details and imaginative concepts has won him the admiration of fashion designers, musicians, film stars, big business heavy-hitters, and international brands.

But for all his worldliness, Jeffrey runs his companies on two basic principles: passion and organization. He realizes the great honor of orchestrating what for some people might be the most important event of their lives, and does all he can to ensure a memorable, unique experience. Whatever Jeffrey Best does, he makes sure to do it as best as he can.

After doing small events for them over the years, the people at GM asked me what they could do to make their cars more fashionable. I came up with the TEN Event, a charity fashion show that pairs top designers with celebrities and GM vehicles. In 2008, it opened the Detroit Auto Show in front of 1,500 members of the press.

Photograph courtesy of Best Events

Photograph courtesy of Best Events

Sean Combs' annual White Party is always one of the most talked about gatherings of the year. With a multi-million dollar French mansion as our starting point, we created white architectural structures to help dominate the surrounding 3.5 acres. The Olympic-sized swimming pool was the centerpiece of the event, so building these structures allowed us to mount lighting to help keep the area inviting after the sun went down. Outdoors or in, private or public, each event has its own vibe and style, so the challenge to make each one perfect is constant.

Photograph courtesy of Best Events

Photograph courtesy of Bart Kresa

Photograph by Jeff Vespa

Photograph by Jeff Vespa

Photograph courtesy of Lighten Up, Inc.

Photograph courtesy of Lighten Up, Inc.

Photograph courtesy of Best Events

Photograph courtesy of Best Events

Above: Interactivity keeps guests from becoming wallflowers. Whether the band descends from the ceiling amid a laser lightshow or your product is readily available for people to experience firsthand, your guests will be more likely to leave feeling like they just attended the most memorable event in ages.

Facing page: The crowd that came to watch the LG Texting Championships needed to be entertained in multiple ways, so we created verticality and tension by modeling the stage after "Who Wants to Be a Millionaire?"

"Being an event planner is akin to being handed a 100-piece jigsaw puzzle, throwing all the pieces in the air, and having to put it together before all the pieces hit the ground."

—Jeffrey Best

Photograph courtesy of Best Events

Photograph courtesy of Best Events

Photograph courtesy of Best Events

"You can't premeditate special moments, but you can think quickly on your feet so you don't get in the way of them."

—Jeffrey Best

Right: A big statement, such as an outdoor logo or extra foliage, can influence an event dramatically. At an Escada launch at The Beverly Wilshire, projecting the brand all over the hotel's exterior created excitement before anyone even went inside. The Academy Awards party thrown by Madonna and Demi Moore created the illusion that the tent was an extension of the house by making it seem as though a terrarium was outside the "windows."

Facing page: Don't be afraid to embrace a theme. A Chanel fashion show debuting the season's "cruise line" of garments wanted to go all out: customized jets, moving walkways, tiered seating that resembled an airport lounge, and a bar that rose from beneath the runway immediately following the show. Ultimately this was more effective than a traditional runway and rows of plastic seats.

Photograph courtesy of Best Events

Photograph courtesy of Best Events

Photograph courtesy of Best Events

Photograph courtesy of Best Events

"I can worry about monogrammed napkins or I can come up with a way to make the experience even more special."

—Jeffrey Best

Right: It would have been silly not to use reclaimed wood at the Environmental Media Awards, and it turned out to be a beautiful, earth-friendly way to reinforce the organization's message.

Facing page: I was encouraged to explore different ideas of a factory for the PlayStation Portable launch, and Andy Warhol's interpretation became the inspiration for the main room. Different vignettes depicting photography, artist, and other types of factories awaited inside.

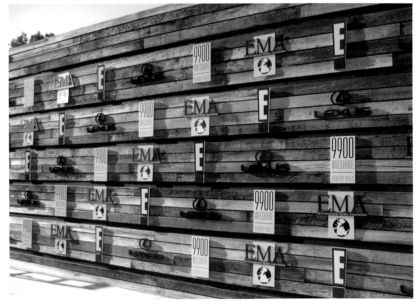

Photograph courtesy of Best Events

views

Let the environment speak to you. All the lights went out at an outdoor wedding I once did, so we gave each guest a votive candle and had them surround the couple while they said their vows. It ultimately doesn't matter about the chairs or sound system, because at the end of the day you can create a special experience with next to nothing if you have to.

BILLY BUTCHKAVITZ DESIGNS

BILLY BUTCHKAVITZ

One of the perks of being a high-end event designer is the opportunity to travel the world. Exotic locales overflow with historic architecture, awe-inspiring flora, and ethnic decorative pieces that captivate you. For Billy Butchkavitz, globe-trotting also offers a unique education, the chance to continually expand his horizons and nurture his inquisitive nature.

It is from these far-flung trips that Billy derives most of his design inspiration. An event designer since 1986, Billy opened his own company two years later and has since developed a loyal following. With the abundant resources of Hollywood's movie and television industry at his fingertips, and his ever-growing catalogue of international artisans and manufacturers to work from, Billy has designed some of Southern California's largest and most impressive events. His team, some of whom have been with him since the 1980s, work their magic to make his visions come spectacularly to life. Billy's brother Brian Butchkavitz, the design and purchasing guru; his sister Peggy Butchkavitz, a whiz with flowers, bookkeeping, and organization; and his best friend J.R. Bryant, the man who keeps the shipping, the expansive warehouse, and the egos all in check, have been with Billy from the beginning.

The goal of a Billy Butchkavitz event is to keep the guests visually entertained, with an underlying goal of also making the host look great. As Billy has found, the key to success and sanity in the event business is to remain diplomatic and flexible—without losing your creative identity.

An HBO Emmy party was inspired largely by the life and work of revolutionary fashion designer Paul Poiret. To emulate his style, an avalanche of patterns and textures took over the Pacific Design Center, which was dominated by a 28-foot-long red chandelier.

Photograph © Gabor Ekecs

Photograph © Gabor Ekecs

Photograph © Gabor Ekecs

Above and left: HBO's dramatization of the Maysles brothers' groundbreaking documentary "Grey Gardens," provided an opportunity to basically design two different parties. In the earlier half of the movie, the mother and daughter are the toast of society, living in splendor on Park Avenue and in their East Hampton mansion. By the end they are dwelling in squalor, two recluses withdrawn from the world. We were provided with all of the movie's costumes, which really helped bring these two worlds to life.

Facing page: We only had 30 hours total to complete the transformation of The Beverly Hilton Hotel's pool and Circa 55 restaurant into an HBO Golden Globes party. Every year this load-in is like a war zone, since our party space is always located next to the awards show space.

Photograph © Gabor Ekecs

Photograph © Gabor Ekecs

Photograph © Gabor Ekecs

Photograph © Gabor Ekecs

Photograph © Gabor Ekecs

"Above all, guests should be visually entertained."

—Billy Butchkavitz

Above and facing page: In the span of one month and using the same fountain location at Paramount Studios, I created three unique HBO premiere parties. The custom round tent for "True Blood," the cabanas for "Hung," and the elevated seating platform for "Entourage" served as key elements for creating these distinct environments.

Previous pages: I was inspired by the architecture of Oscar Niemeyer and the city of Brasilia when designing an HBO Emmy party that showcased original art from South American artists. The 27-foot diameter silver chandelier was an homage to Niemeyer.

Photograph © Gabor Ekecs

Photograph © Gabor Ekecs

Photograph © Gabor Ekecs

Photograph © Gabor Ekecs

Photograph © Gabor Ekecs

Photograph © Gabor Ekecs

"Everybody, from the chef to the lighting tech to the set builder, has a bit of wisdom or trick-of-the-trade that can help you in the long run. Ask questions, listen, and learn."

—Billy Butchkavitz

Right: Outside of the Pacific Design Center, a custom turquoise tent and replicas of an Indian pavilion brought the city of Jaipur to life in California. While gathering ideas in India, it took incredible self-control not to buy everything I saw!

Facing page: To bring a sense of authenticity, a majority of the décor pieces were manufactured in Thailand. Getting everything to the site on time was a massive challenge, but the resulting effect was nothing short of spectacular. Invoking the beauty of Thailand, the colors and patterns worked in harmony, from the carpet to the tablecloths to even the custom tinted tent. A 25-foot-tall golden Buddha statue stood watch over the evening.

Photograph © Gabor Ekecs

views

I never forget that I am in the service industry. I am not the host—I'm the designer they hired to work for them. In this business, your life revolves around the host: their schedule, their needs, their likes and dislikes. It's up to me to absorb it all and steer them down the path of good taste.

SEQUOIA PRODUCTIONS

CHERYL CECCHETTO | GARY LEVITT

Sequoia Productions, led by founder and president Cheryl Cecchetto, is at the apex of its profession. Cheryl and her elite team of super planners have succeeded in producing and designing some of the most luminary events in the business, including the Academy Awards Governors Ball for 20 years and the Primetime Emmys Governors Ball for 12. Working alongside vice president Gary Levitt and their dream team staff, Sequoia brings to bear highly seasoned technical, managerial, and people skills that have blazed a trail of innovative technology, creative originality, and impeccable boutique service. The key to the company's success lies in its fierce reputation for demanding only the highest of expectations from each host and delivering that much more.

Sequoia's reputation appears to crop up in all the right circles. An ability to instill confidence and trust, coupled with creative savvy and technical expertise, has long been its trademark. Dedication to this ideal has garnished a clientele both national and international, who remain staunch regulars, some for over two decades running.

The subject of numerous television and radio interviews, as well as a featured speaker at many national annual event gatherings, Cheryl is the quintessential "dame" of the event industry. Her book *Obsessed to Create* is an insightful look at her adventures in the high-profile event world. But beneath it all, her small town Canadian roots run deep, and her resolute work ethic and down-to-earth candor remain her guiding light, as she and Sequoia Productions continue to grow, slow and steady, and judging by the company's reputation, majestic as well.

The 57th Primetime Emmy Awards® Governors Ball was modeled after the grand SS Normandie, a 1930s luxury ocean liner. The goal was to recreate the opulent splendor—the luxury and romance—that was the essence of this grand liner, and I believe the goal was accomplished.

Photograph by Nadine Froger Photography

Photograph by Line 8 Photography

Photograph by Line 8 Photography

Above: The designer grand staircase ascending to the orchestra balcony was the room's focal point. Cigar girls and waitstaff dressed in period originals designed by Jeffrey Kurland added an element of living nostalgia to the festivities.

Right: An exclusive new addition was the Oscar Engraving Service Area, aka "Oscar Workshop." For the first time ever, Academy Award winners could have their statuettes engraved at the Governors Ball immediately following the ceremony.

Facing page: The theme for the 82nd Academy Awards® Governors Ball was a swank 1930s supper club. Cecchetto's design was inspired by such icons as Paul Williams and Dorothy Draper. The uniquely curved and tiered ceiling treatment and stylized beaded and fiber optic chandelier captured beautifully the distinct nostalgia of that era. No less impressive was the innovative use of floral, fabric, and lighting design to create the opulent standard of that time.

Photograph by Line 8 Photography

Photograph by Line 8 Photography

"The goal is not to create an event, but an experience, one that lives on in the memory of the guest long after they've gone home."

—Cheryl Cecchetto

Above: The décor at Citrus was so elegantly beautiful, we hated to remove it. Instead, we layered the existing interior design with polished enhancements and stylized imagination. Voila! Instant enchantment.

Facing page top left: The challenge in branding is discovering how to strike an aesthetic balance between product icon and décor. A stylized Sequoia "step and repeat" at the guest entrance brilliantly highlighted the distant Hollywood skyline.

Facing page bottom left: Emirates introduced the newest, largest Airbus of its kind. We produced an oversized banner that blended the beauty of the Kodak Theatre's façade with the sleek style of the Airbus A380, an effect that proved entreating but not distracting.

Facing page right: *Entertainment Weekly*'s annual Pre-Emmy Celebration was certainly one of the most popular events we've produced. It was an exclusive affair that featured a guest list of who's who, and required a uniquely subtle yet powerful display of branding.

Photograph by Nadine Froger Photography

Photograph by Nadine Froger Photography

Photograph by Nadine Froger Photography

Photograph by ZenTodd.com

Photograph by ZenTodd.com

"Bigger budgets and higher guest counts doth not a great event make."
—Cheryl Cecchetto

Right: An outside ceremony displayed natural beauty, which added to the emotional serenity of the evening. The woodsy background, the lush greenery—it was exquisite.

Facing page: We created an indoor event outdoors, with willow trees draped in crystal chandeliers and candlelight dining beneath a ceiling of jeweled stars. Musicians gently played, framed by a backdrop of open-air night sky. The entire evening was dreamlike and intimate, like a lullaby.

views

The real party is in the details. Even after you've set your budget, theme, guest count, and décor, the real work has yet to begin. Discovering those moments of guest experience is what makes the difference between a good party and an extraordinary event. It may be in the way the overhead lighting cascades onto the table overlay or in the stylized seating arrangements. In any case, it's these kinds of subtle discoveries that forge truly vivid memories. So take the time to celebrate the details and you'll create a truly unforgettable event.

CARAVENTS
CARA KLEINHAUT

While at Sony Music Entertainment in New York City for eight years, Cara Kleinhaut worked with some of the world's most demanding artists and executives, perfecting her skills in production management fundamentals such as staging, sound, lighting and environmental design, talent management, and logistics. After her tenure there she took those skills and her natural gift for inventiveness and founded Caravents in 2001. Now a featured producer of major award shows, lifestyle and celebrity events for leading brands, and select social gatherings, Caravents has enjoyed a steady rise to the top because of its ability to service hosts in a wide variety of industries, from publishing to luxury goods and beyond. Its award-winning in-house visual media team is responsible for some of the most exciting and original lifestyle and brand imagery in the business.

Known for combining stimulating visual media with beautifully detailed environments, Caravents has built its reputation on dealing with the creative and strategic side of production as much as the logistical side of planning. Through this, guests, tastemakers, and the media all experience a hands-on, cohesive design that fully immerses guests in the brand and all it has to offer.

With offices in both Los Angeles and New York, Caravents is available throughout the United States and abroad. A slew of prestigious event awards, continuous high-profile presence, and relationships with prominent, leading brands such as Target and Time Inc. have created a successful base for Caravents to continue its growth as an innovator in imaginative, experiential design.

The Independent Spirit Awards, formerly held on the beach, was staged for the first time in 2010 in downtown Los Angeles at LA Live. We turned a tent on a parking lot roof into a sexy, glam nightclub for the *ELLE* green room, making it a celebrity retreat decked in platinum and mirror mosaic, white suede, and black lacquer. A variety of sponsors were artfully styled into one cohesive overall event design, ultimately reflecting the *ELLE* brand, where select advertiser products were displayed and gifted to celebrities while guests and media lounged and sipped champagne in a relaxed, party setting.

Photograph by Line 8 Photography

Photograph by Line 8 Photography

Above and left: After producing a number of high-profile award shows, we know that a tight, well-styled show that runs on time is the number one priority. The 2009 *ELLE* Women in Hollywood Awards, hosted by Alec Baldwin, featured such honorees as Julie Andrews and Reneé Zellweger. It was a high-powered dinner sponsored by Calvin Klein, so we completely transformed the Four Seasons ballroom into a sleek and minimalist space, accented with bright pops of red and fuchsia.

Facing page top: For the award-winning 2009 *InStyle* Golden Globes suites showcasing jewelry, accessories, and cosmetics, we transformed three regular conference rooms and lawn space at the Four Seasons Hotel Los Angeles into luxury atelier experiences that transcended regular gifting rooms. Gracing the cover of BizBash's national print edition and winning a prestigious design award at The Special Event convention, winning over submissions from event companies around the globe, the space was truly gorgeous.

Facing page bottom: When Converse launched its One Star brand exclusively for Target, the theme was youthful, hip, and cutting-edge. Our creative visual media team created an interactive, 60-foot video wall featuring an evolving photo wall activation. Throughout the night, people could have their pictures taken and our on-site graphic designers would use movement and special effects to integrate them into the constantly changing video wall, making every guest a star. Many have tried to replicate the experience, but it is a signature installation we are very proud of, using the unique skill set of our in-house media team.

Photograph by Line 8 Photography

"Every design decision and production detail influences the environment and ambience, and the collection of those details is what events, or branded experiences, are all about."

—Cara Kleinhaut

Photograph by Line 8 Photography

Photograph by Line 8 Photography

Photograph by Line 8 Photography

Photograph by Line 8 Photography

Photograph by Simone & Martin Photography

Photograph by Kerry Kara Photography

"Of course guests should enjoy the event, but the person who should be having the most fun is the host."
—Cara Kleinhaut

Right: At a private estate wedding in Montecito, the hosts didn't want the backyard to be a sea of predictable round tables. By constructing specialty dining cabanas and interactive food stations, guests were encouraged to mix, mingle, and enjoy the spectacular ocean views.

Facing page: The weddings we produce are usually for couples who want something more than what they would see in a typical bridal magazine. We are particularly proud of the close relationships and honor of being an "agency partner," not just a vendor, for our return hosts. For example *Essence* magazine has asked us to produce its signature program during Oscar week, the Black Women in Hollywood Awards, every year since it started. The event has been held in The Beverly Hills Hotel's Crystal Ballroom and garden, where we re-create a new style and theme for each year.

Photograph by Line 8 Photography

views

Creating an immersive environment for people is the essence of what we do. It is always thrilling to see guests and clients having a positive experience within our events. From planning to execution there are literally thousands of details, but to see it all come together into one experience is extremely satisfying. What makes it work is a complete team approach. The entire Caravents team has true passion for their work and brings their A game and unique talent to every project. If you have a passion for something, it will be a success.

Event Eleven

TONY SCHUBERT

Tony Schubert will readily admit he has an amazing job. As the founder and owner of Event Eleven, he gets to produce large-scale, multi-themed, interactive events for practically every heavy-hitter in both the entertainment and corporate worlds. His high-profile blockbuster film premieres, designer fashion shows, celebrity award show afterparties, brand-name product launches, and memorable weddings are known for combining cutting-edge, modern ideas with clean, beautiful accents. But for Tony, it's not about celebrities and the glittering circles they travel in; it's the unique challenge of taking a normal, everyday space and magically transforming it into a temporary dream world that truly excites him.

After spending years investing in and promoting his friends' nightclubs in Los Angeles, Tony decided to take the leap and produce his now annual Halloween bash in Hollywood. That event's success was only the tipping point. In 1997, when he was only 24, Tony launched Event Eleven, naming his company in tribute to the street he'd grown up on and as a nod to his late mother. In the years that followed, Event Eleven snagged the First Annual Latin Grammy Awards, both the debut fashion show and afterparty for pop star Justin Timberlake's William Rast clothing line at Los Angeles Fashion Week, and the 2009 and 2010 post-SAG Awards galas. For these, as with every event he produces, Tony maintains that intense planning and forethought are the true cornerstones of his remarkable work.

The SAG gala hosted by *People* magazine is known for being a lavish event, and we did not disappoint in 2010. Instead of going the traditional route and draping the 100-foot-long tent entirely in fabric, we confined the blue-green organdy to the ceiling and built birch walls treated with a blue stain. At varying heights we hung 400 Edison light bulbs, then interspersed 27 Plexiglass globes filled with purple hydrangeas and orchids that dangled from clear fishing line, making it look as though they were floating in mid-air. The neutral vinyl-covered furniture was recycled from last year's bash in order to support SAG's green initiatives.

Photograph by Nadine Froger Photography

Photograph by Nadine Froger Photography

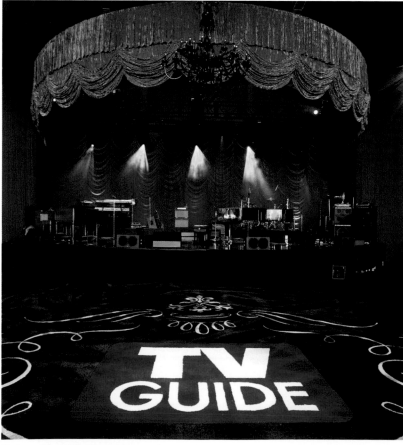

Above and left: The French burlesque vibe of Hollywood nightclub Les Deux—which I also designed—was the perfect inspiration for the 5th Annual *TV Guide* Party celebrating the Emmy winners and nominees. A sensuous deep red, gold, and black color scheme balanced neatly with the delicately trimmed hedges and juniper trees of the open-air French garden. I kept the flow seamless by connecting the club to the tent with hedged arbor passageways lit by hanging black crystal chandeliers.

Facing page: It's a terrific challenge to produce the same event year after year, because you absolutely cannot recycle ideas or details. If you look at the first year I took over the SAG Gala and then compare it to the second, the differences are striking, but both events are luxurious and memorable in their own way.

Photograph by Nadine Froger Photography

"What can you do to make your guests stop dead in their tracks and say 'Wow'? That should always be the first question."

—Tony Schubert

Photograph by Nadine Froger Photography

Photograph by Nadine Froger Photography

Photograph by Line 8 Photography

Photograph by Line 8 Photography

Photograph by Nadine Froger Photography

Photograph by Nadine Froger Photography

"Inspiration can strike at any time, even when you're just walking down the street."

—Tony Schubert

Right: Amber tones and ruffled florals were grounded by budding tree branches at a private wedding.

Facing page top: Metallic surfaces reflected the sleek silver and black color palette, and futuristic floral tabletop centerpieces added a pop of color at the "Star Trek" feature film premiere afterparty.

Facing page bottom: In 2006, the Museum of Contemporary Art presented a retrospective of the work of Robert Rauschenberg. For the opening gala, I took my cues from the artist's photographs, paintings, and sculptures, creating a provocative space that hinted at Rauschenberg's proclivity for pop art.

Photograph by Nadine Froger Photography

views

My foolproof tip? Lighting. You can completely transform your venue with amber light bulbs, dimmers, candlelight—anything that softens rough edges and creates a velvety glow makes people look instantly sexier.

J. BEN BOURGEOIS PRODUCTIONS, INC.

Splashed across a contemporary painting in Ben Bourgeois' personal collection are the words "Be Amazing." He loves the constant reminder to push himself—and his J. Ben Bourgeois Productions team—beyond the unthinkable. With a mantra like that, it's hard not to have a great attitude, even when insane requests are routinely thrown their way. Everyone agrees that Ben has one of those rare magnetic personalities that just inspires people to outdo themselves.

Since establishing his high-energy company in 1990, Ben has produced events for major fashion designers, businesses, museums, and a host of affluent private patrons—and left their guests in utter amazement. "Challenge us!" is the company's open-ended invitation to corporate moguls, social divas, and everyone in-between. Confident in his team's abilities to wow even the most discerning hosts, Ben thrives on tight parameters and unfamiliar situations, always rising to the occasion.

Southern California's special event scene is one of the most intense and impressive in the world, and Ben is proud to be at the forefront. He and his team are, indeed, amazing and quite enthusiastic about their careers, which filters positive energy to the vendors and, ultimately, the guests. They are big picture people with extraordinary attention to detail and an uncanny ability to weave together all of the components that make events spectacular.

The Orange County Performing Arts Center is the country's largest non-profit arts organization, so the grand opening of the Renée and Henry Segerstrom Concert Hall had to be impactful within the arts community. A custom clear tent was created to allow over 1,100 guests the perfect view of the concert hall as well as the stunning Richard Serra installation.

Photograph by Nadine Froger Photography

Photograph by Line 8 Photography

Photograph by Nadine Froger Photography

Photograph by Nadine Froger Photography

"Putting a clever twist on a traditional element is the simplest way to engage the widest audience."
—J. Ben Bourgeois

I always design an element of surprise in my productions—a quick second of drama that takes your breath away. Whether it's revealing the Van Cleef & Arpels California rêverie collection within a 55-foot video wall or dropping a 160-foot wall to reveal the Broad Contemporary Museum, there should always be at least one moment that leaves guests speechless. We keep our ideas fresh and our organizational skills sharp by being involved in everything from cultural events like the International Friends of the Louvre gala in Paris to lavish private dinner parties.

Photograph by Nadine Froger Photography

Photograph by Line 8 Photography

Photograph by Nadine Froger Photography

Photograph by Nadine Froger Photography

Photograph by Nadine Froger Photography

It's both exciting and exhausting to travel all over the world producing events. Mexico City, Paris, London, Venice, Tokyo—we've found ourselves in places ranging from romantic and exotic to really remote. We're always happy to have events in our own backyard because Southern California is one of the friendliest, most beautiful places on earth. The Wallis Annenberg Space for Photography opening, Donatella Versace's Fire & Ice ball, galas for the Louis Vuitton United Cancer Front, and a private dinner for Rémy Cointreau are a few of our favorite grand-scale events.

Photograph by Nadine Froger Photography

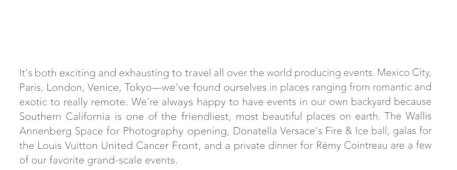

views

The most efficient way to produce an event is with a small, core team of experts whose talents and dedication to every production is unmatched in the industry. This maximizes adaptability and ensures the right mix of people collaborating on the host's behalf. We select the best professionals for the best results given any set of circumstances.

WENDY CREED PRODUCTIONS

WENDY CREED

Los Angeles is a town that thrives on entertainment; from award shows to film premieres to nightclubs, there is always another "opening night" to attend. As a former actor, there is no one better to understand the importance of entertainment and drama than Wendy Creed. Classically trained at the Old Vic Theatre School in England, Wendy's career took her to the stage and screen in both New York and Canada. A period of purveying antique silver, glass, and home accessories through Creeds, her family's fashion emporium, fulfilled her other creative side, and the inception of Wendy Creed Productions was not far behind.

A full-service event production and environments firm, Wendy's company has produced high-profile celebrations for everything from movie premieres to celebrity weddings to sports-related shindigs. In the last decade, she has staged 10 Super Bowl events for the NFL, as well as designed the impossibly chic Hollywood nightclubs Lobby and Privilege. Fashion, professional sports, entertainment, interior design, Fortune 500 companies, beauty—no matter the intended audience, Wendy's hands-on style and team of professionals continually deliver modern, original productions full of visionary talent, cutting-edge style, and impeccable service.

Wendy is known for intuitively recognizing a host's personality and lifestyle, then translating that individual "brand" into a memorable event bursting with incomparable style. Perhaps her theatrical background plays a part in her ability to create entire worlds for one magical evening. Or perhaps she's just very good at what she does.

Directly inspired by the event "Creative Reflections" for Mercedes-Benz Fashion Week, the design for the Star Lounge transformed it from a white box into a mirrored world. The reflection of the models in the car photographs, along with floor-to-ceiling mirrors and small mirrored touches in the tables, vases, and lamps, created 360 degrees of reflections.

Photograph by Silvia Mautner

Photograph by Cindy Gold & Claudia Wong

Photograph by Silvia Mautner

Photograph by Joe Fornabaio

Photograph by Silvia Mautner

Photograph by Silvia Mautner

Right: We turned an airplane hangar into the ultimate Officers Club for the NFL Super Bowl XXXVII Friday Night Party. Our post-modern reception began within a canopied garden, where fragrant flowers and lush foliage framed an "outdoor living room."

Facing page: It's always fun to transform a space into something entirely unexpected. An empty warehouse was converted into a mid-century home for a sweet sixteen party, complete with orange shag carpeting and disco balls. For another event, we covered a private backyard swimming pool to create more usable seating space. All the furniture and design elements were inspired by natural materials: blonde wood, grasscloth wall panels with shelves of green apples, glass troughs of wheatgrass and candlelight.

Previous pages left: As guests walked through the gates of the Wonka Factory for the premiere of the Warner Bros. film "Charlie and the Chocolate Factory," they were met with grassy hills and valleys, accented by candy cane trees, lollipop bushes, polka-dotted mushrooms, and sugar-glazed pumpkins.

Previous pages top: For the premiere of "Harry Potter and the Order of the Phoenix," we creatively moved guests from a courtyard evocative of the Forbidden Forest inside by recreating the film's Floo Network with an oversized fireplace and emerald green flame projections. Inside awaited a replica of the Great Hall's enchanted ceiling, a wall decked with orbs emulated the Hall of Prophecies, and there were even kitten-decorated china plates from Dolores Umbridge's office, complete with meowing sound effects, to decorate the restrooms.

Previous pages bottom: High above the real Gotham City, the 36th-floor ballroom of the Mandarin Oriental Hotel had all the airs of an elite penthouse party for the premiere of "The Dark Knight," with one small catch: We covered the room in the Joker's taunting red graffiti. "Reserved" signs were slashed with Xs, "Ha Ha Ha" decorated almost every window, and a wall of flat-screen televisions featured imagery from the film with eyes crossed out and insulting messages smeared across them. It was as if the Joker had crashed the party himself.

Photograph by Silvia Mautner

views

It's easy to get swept up in the big picture, but remember the small details. Something that seems obvious to you might delight your guests with its unique ability to capture personality and individuality.

Location, Loca

PELICAN HILL RESORT

GEORGE NICKELS

It may have only been open since late 2008, but Pelican Hill Resort® feels like it's been there for centuries. Fully grown, mature trees dot the 504 acres of property, situated perfectly along the Newport Coast. Tuscan design, heavily influenced by the great Italian Renaissance architect Andrea Palladio, invokes Old World European charm. And extensive attention to detail—both on its property and in its service—elevates the resort to a whole new level of magnificence.

So it's no surprise that Pelican Hill Resort is often the top choice for couples and companies looking to host a truly spectacular event. George Nickels, the resort's director of weddings, reveals that the trinity of hotel, golf course, and private estate is what makes Pelican Hill Resort so attractive to potential hosts, especially those looking to plan a destination celebration. George, along with his director of catering and conference services Beni Vines, makes certain that every host and guest is awed by the resort's splendor.

With 204 spacious bungalows and 128 full-service villas, lavish living space abounds. But the resort's multiple event spaces, ranging from outdoor terraces to dramatic ballrooms to a separate private estate, are an irresistible draw. To guarantee undivided attention, Pelican Hill Resort only hosts one wedding per day. Besides eliminating the chance that any details might slip by, this allows the passionate and highly trained staff to focus on what they do best: help create astonishingly beautiful memories.

Our iconic Italian-style rotunda is perched 300 feet above the ocean and offers panoramic views of the Pacific and two Tom Fazio-designed golf courses. The oval infinity edge garden, known as the Event Lawn, completes the magical outdoor setting, perfect for enjoying a sunset or gazing at nearby Catalina Island.

Photograph by Tom Lamb

Photograph by Marshall Williams

Photograph by Shannon Treglia

Photograph by Mike Colon

Above, right, and facing page: Well thought out details, such as floor-to-ceiling windows, iron chandeliers, and a spectacular limestone fireplace, lend dramatic elegance to the Mar Vista Ballroom. The room's terrace, with its hand-tiled fountain and outdoor fireplace, is another way for guests to enjoy the nearly perfect year-round weather.

Previous pages: The Coliseum Pool, designed to resemble its namesake in Rome, is the world's largest full-circle swimming pool, measuring 136 feet in diameter and featuring over 1 million glass tiles. In addition to plenty of cushioned poolside lounge chairs, 18 cabanas featuring HD flat-screen televisions and Bose stereo systems make for decadent hideaways.

Photograph by Eric Figge

Photograph by Marshall Williams

Photograph by Marshall Williams

Photograph by Marshall Williams

Photograph by Marshall Williams

Mar Vista is almost like its own entity. Guests still have full access to the wonderful amenities on the main property, but the location, set aside from the hotel with a private entrance and dedicated space for hosts to relax before the big event, makes it feel like you are hosting a party in your own private estate. The luxury service standard is one server for every 15 guests, but here we insist on one for every 10. The synchronized service we offer, with plates being distributed directly from the kitchen, makes it possible for meals to be served even while speeches or presentations are occurring. The in-house culinary team strives not only to create delicious food, but to present it in innovative ways, too. Cocktail sauce poured into an ice block, for example, is both functional and unexpected.

Photograph by Mike Colón

Photograph by Marshall Williams

Photograph by Marshall Williams

Photograph by Marshall Williams

Photograph by Marshall Williams

"You can build a beautiful property, but it's the people who work there that make all the difference."
—George Nickels

Right and facing page: With the rotunda as a backdrop, sometimes a simple sprinkling of butter yellow rose petals and hints of raspberry red are all it takes to make a statement. One of the hallmarks of Pelican Hill Resort is its versatility. The resort is stunning without any décor, but its classic Italian-inspired architecture also blends incredibly well with the most elaborate design scheme.

Previous pages: The breathtaking ocean views and rolling golf course greens are only a part of the resort's grandeur. To make use of the incredible weather, one company turned its event's reception into an Italian festa, a street fair celebrating the bounties of the earth. Stilt-walkers, market stalls, and hired actors transformed the resort into another world.

Photograph by Joe Photo

views

California has so many stunning places to hold an event that it sometimes makes choosing just one overwhelming. The very first feeling you get upon arriving is your indicator. Notice how every staff member treats you—after all, your guests probably won't be interacting with the sales manager. Not every property is right for every person, but as soon as the valet opens the door, you should know if it is right for you.

MONTAGE BEVERLY HILLS

The meaning of montage is "an artful compilation," which serves as the inspiration for Montage Hotels & Resorts as envisioned by founder and CEO Alan Fuerstman. Beginning with the flagship Montage Laguna Beach, Montage Hotels & Resorts is a collection of masterpieces that offer stunning settings, impeccable hospitality, and memorable culinary, spa, and lifestyle experiences. Seven years in the making, Montage Beverly Hills personifies the artistry of Montage.

Steps from Rodeo Drive, in the heart of the Golden Triangle, Montage Beverly Hills is the first high-end hotel to grace Beverly Hills in 17 years and the only new California hotel to receive the prestigious 2010 *Forbes* Five Star Award. Along with 201 guestrooms, including 55 suites, this urban oasis offers award-winning cuisine, a 20,000-square-foot spa, rooftop pool, and 9,000 square feet of special event space.

Personalized service is a hallmark of the Montage culture, delivered with a refreshing blend of European graciousness and American style. What sets this enigmatic hotel apart from its Beverly Hills predecessors? Finely tuned services that adapt to 21st century needs, such as flexible check-in and checkout; a high associate-to-guest ratio; the assurance that only one large event is booked per day; astute touches like custom china and linens; and a passion for culinary excellence demonstrated through custom-designed menus. Montage Hotels & Resorts also employs a permanent director of learning, resulting in highly intuitive associates that are in the moment and well-versed in the art of the "wow" factor.

Inspired by the simplicity of European gardens, the Beverly Canon Gardens present a respite of fountains, benches, and pedestrian galleries across from Bouchon, Thomas Keller's famed French bistro.

Photograph by Scott Frances

Photograph by Yitzhak Dalal Photography

Photograph by Yitzhak Dalal Photography

Montage Beverly Hills' enviable address renders it the perfect place to celebrate life's most memorable moments, from a social ceremony to a corporate gathering. The hotel can accommodate both small soirées and glamorous galas in the 5,000-square-foot Marquesa ballroom, a Spanish Colonial-inspired haven flaunting romantic opera-style balconies, richly upholstered walls, majestic chandeliers, and elegant décor, suitable for up to 320 seated guests. The 3,000-square-foot Contessa room lends an elegant ambience for up to 210 seated guests, with its gracefully appointed furnishings and estate-quality wall coverings. For a cocktail reception, the 1,200-square-foot glass-enclosed rooftop Conservatory Dining Room, ideal for up to 70 seated guests, features dramatic views of the cityscape. Guest lists receive the utmost discretion thanks to a separate arrival and reception area.

"Gazing upon the famed Hollywood Hills, awash in natural light or under the night sky, is an idyllic setting for an intimate outdoor ceremony."

—Shaun Brown

Our talented chefs and sommeliers are a testament to Montage Beverly Hills' unparalleled appreciation for fine food and wine and penchant for earning the industry's top accolades. True culinary artisans are trained to surprise and delight with creative menus that showcase the freshest regional and seasonal ingredients, signature Montage cocktails, housemade smoothies, wine pairings from our extensive cellars, and custom cakes. We feature an array of dining options from casually elegant to highly refined, sure to impress the most discriminating palates with classic California-inspired dishes and modern French fare.

Photograph by Yitzhak Dalal Photography

Photograph by Christina Dominguez for Joe Buissink

Photograph by Christina Dominguez for Joe Buissink

"The marriage of vintage Hollywood style and modern sophistication creates a fairytale backdrop for new vows and promises renewed."
—Darrell Schmitt

Our impeccable team of event specialists ensures that every wedding is a masterpiece. With only one wedding per day, wedding parties are assured paramount attention, as Montage Beverly Hills associates fulfill every spoken and unspoken need. A selection of romantic spaces reflects the city's glamour estates of the Golden Era. Rehearsal dinners, bridal showers, and wedding brunches can be rendered to reflect any theme. We can arrange salon services and spa treatments, like a couple's massage to ease pre-ceremony jitters, and provide recommendations for a who's who of wedding professionals. Destination weddings are a specialty, with every detail flawlessly orchestrated, from accommodations to complete weekend itineraries for visiting friends and family.

Photograph by Christina Dominguez for Joe Buissink

Photograph by Christina Dominguez for Joe Buissink

"The perfect mix of setting and service creates a canvas for artful gatherings. Nothing celebrates life quite like a marvelous party with friends and family."

—Alan Fuerstman

From anniversaries and dinners to birthdays and retirement parties, social events at Montage Beverly Hills embody the spirit of the occasion. Intimate affairs may be reserved at a variety of convivial dining venues: Parq's interactive Chef's Table, the Muse patio or private dining room, or the rooftop Conservatory Dining Room. Each space offers a level of service, cuisine, and privacy rivaling Beverly Hills' most sought-after tables. Overnight guests are treated to distinctive amenities, including the two-story Spa Montage with 17 treatment rooms, private mineral pools, the full-service Kim Vo Salon, and the rooftop pool with panoramic views. Quite simply, our property is a new art form that assembles the traditions of its iconic setting to transform every event into an artful experience.

Photograph by Christina Dominguez for Joe Buissink

views

Montage Beverly Hills is the first ultra-luxury hotel in Southern California to receive LEED Gold certification. Besides extensive recycling programs and conscious limiting of energy, more than 25 percent of the building materials were sourced locally, and the proximity to nearby chic neighborhoods makes walking or cycling a viable option for guests.

[SEVEN-DEGREES]

The number "7" conjures up many associations: seven days of the week, the Seven Wonders of the World, lucky number seven. For art and event venue [seven-degrees], the number refers mainly to the architectural angles found within the building's design. Nestled in the arts district of Laguna Beach, the two-building, 25,000-square-foot space houses not only indoor and outdoor locations specifically built for entertaining, but also an art gallery and artists' live-work studios.

Open since 2001, [seven-degrees] is a blank canvas equipped with all the necessary tools to create a personalized masterpiece. The in-house team of event experts can handle all design, planning, and production, as well as catering, florals, and décor. The 4,500-square-foot Media Lounge, with its constantly rotating art exhibits, is chameleon-like in its versatility. A fully integrated LED lighting system, zoned sound system, mounted flat-panel video displays, retractable large-screen video projection systems, and live feed video cameras give hosts a wide array of technological toys to play with. Even the outdoor areas—a hillside terrace, a creative use of balcony space—are one-of-a-kind.

The team at [seven-degrees], led by executive director Dora Wexell, employs a collaborative approach with its hosts, involving them in the process and coaxing out their inner artistes. The resident artists also occasionally weigh in, bringing their imagination and unique perspective to the table. Teamwork is only one of the venue's set of elements, which also includes emphasis on design, technology, and connection. How many elements in total? Seven, of course.

DeeDee Anderson and Mark Orgill, co-founders of [seven-degrees], bought the property, designed the space, and spent over three years building it. The outcome is a fresh and entirely original approach to art and celebrations—it's like a big sculpture that's constantly changing.

Photograph by David Tosti

Photograph by David Tosti

Photograph by David Tosti

Photograph by David Tosti

Heather Gaughan and Brandy Valdez, [seven-degrees] partners and daughters of co-founder DeeDee Anderson, surprised DeeDee with a 60th birthday party that was unlike anything we'd ever done before. DeeDee travels a lot, so the exotic glamour of Asia held both personal significance and a gorgeous design opportunity. Raj Tents transformed our long driveway into a regal red carpet entrance, leis imported from Malaysia hung from custom-welded frames bolted to the tables, and Wayne Foster Music & Entertainment wrote a special song about DeeDee in addition to rocking the party all evening long.

Photograph by David Tosti

Photograph by David Tosti

"This space was designed for the building to settle into the background, allowing the event itself to really pop."

—Dora Wexell

The orientation of the Media Lounge is so easy to adjust; there is no set "front of the room." And while the space is large, what makes it feel even larger is the reflective ceiling, always a nice touch to reflect candlelight and color.

Photograph by David Tosti

Photograph by David Tosti

Photograph by David Tosti

Photograph by David Tosti

"You could attend an event here every night and swear you're never in the same location."

—Dora Wexell

Right: The terrace flows freely from the interior of the building, allowing for an even greater sense of openness. Scrolling up the side of the hill is a three-tiered garden complete with bamboo walkways and a waterfall.

Facing page: Unlike a lot of venues, we don't have a set design sensibility. You don't have to work with our existing colors or adjust your ideas to fit around what can't be changed. We like to say we are a blank canvas—practically everything can be changed!

Photograph by David Tosti

views

Since the building was designed specifically as an art and event venue, it contains a lot of thoughtful details that make everyone's lives easier. Electrical outlets are everywhere, it's already wired and set up for sound and projection, we have an established system for quickly hanging and replacing artwork—little logistical things you may not think about initially end up being the difference between a harried event and a smooth one.

THE BEVERLY HILTON

SANDY MURPHY

A "star" was born in 1955 as distinguished hotelier Conrad Hilton broke ground on his flagship West Coast property, laying the foundation for what would become one of the most prestigious and important venues for Hollywood. Over the years, The Beverly Hilton has hosted the inaugural Grammy Awards, the American Film Institute Lifetime Achievement Awards, and has served as the home of the Hollywood Foreign Press Association's Golden Globe Awards Show and the Academy of Motion Picture Arts & Sciences Oscar Nominations Luncheon. Beny Alagem and Oasis West Realty LLC purchased The Beverly Hilton in late 2003 from its previous owner, entertainer Merv Griffin, immediately embarking on an $80 million reinvention of the nine-acre property. The star-studded guest register has always included the world's most recognizable names, celebrities drawn by the hotel's glamorous mystique and four-star service. Today, as a direct result of Beny's vision and comprehensive reinvention, the "star" is reborn.

The Beverly Hilton is the largest hotel production facility in Beverly Hills, offering more than 60,000 square feet of upscale indoor and open-air event space on the lobby level, plus thousands of square feet on the rooftop. The versatile platforms make the possibilities endless for event planners.

When it first opened, the hotel greeted its guests with a 500-pound starburst created by artist Bernard Rosenthal in the main lobby. A portion of the original sculpture, a symbol of space and freedom, remains on display by the Oasis Pool as a little piece of tangible history.

The architecture of Luis Barragan and vintage '60s textiles provided the inspiration for HBO's 2009 Golden Globes After-Party. Event designer Billy Butchkavitz washed the space in banana yellow and chocolate brown, with 20-foot-high yellow walls, reproduction period furniture, and outdoor lounge areas with glass and chrome firepits. The citrine lighting and moving images within HBO's logo on an animal print wall were courtesy of Images by Lighting and Bart Kresa. Executive Hotel Chef Katsuo Sugiura created a menu of passed hors d'oeuvres and buffets including salmon cakes on crispy wonton skin, smoked duck with grilled pineapple, and truffled mac and cheese.

Photograph © Gabor Ekecs

Photograph by Line 8 Photography

Photograph by Nadine Froger Photography

"Events of global importance need to be held in settings with global prominence."

—Sandy Murphy

Right: On the hotel's opening day, members of the press were the first guests to taste the "Starburst Cocktail" while looking out over the Hollywood Hills from Star on the Roof, one of Beverly Hills' first rooftop bars. Today, the hotel has a similar signature drink called the "Startini" that is served at special occasions on what is now the Stardust Rooftop event space. For a star-studded birthday celebration, the host wanted a seamless flow from indoors to outdoors, surrounded by the night sky. The hotel's catering specialist designed décor of pure white accented with breakout patterns of purple and pink.

Facing page: The Beverly Hilton's Oasis Courtyard took on a French theme for *InStyle* and Warner Bros. Studio's 10th annual Golden Globes viewing and afterparty. The French-style motif was overseen of Time Inc.'s Cyd Wilson and designed by Thomas Ford in shades of magenta, burgundy, and silver with bright red rose-topped tables .

Previous pages: Cartier, a sponsor at NBC's Golden Globes viewing and afterparty, showcased jewels and baubles from its vault in Paris, making for dazzling décor against the metallic and black look created by Angel City Designs. Bright white flower arrangements of hydrangeas, lilies, roses, and tulips complemented the black walls, orange-toned lighting, and clusters of black chandeliers.

Photograph by Dustin Engelskind, Obsidian Productions

views

Holding an event at a location known for its rich history adds a special extra layer to the festivities. World famous film stars, politicians, and personalities have walked The Beverly Hilton's halls and even the name conjures up images of glamour and sophistication. Every event is magical, but celebrating where John F. Kennedy and Frank Sinatra once did gives the whole experience an extra touch.

Terranea Resort

Tracy Koven

Choosing the location for your special event is the first, and arguably most important, decision in the whole planning process. It reflects your personal aesthetic and immediately establishes the tone of the event. When the location embodies Pacific coast style with a Mediterranean spirit and includes lush scenery, the tranquil sound of waves crashing into the California coastline, exquisite indoor-outdoor ballrooms, and amenities galore, it's hard to go wrong in any subsequent decisions—that's what you call peace of mind.

With 270-degree ocean views and Catalina Island across the way, Terranea Resort is a unique haven that easily inspires turning a simple day-trip for an event or meeting into a much longer respite. From enjoying nature-inspired spa treatments or whale-watching to teeing off toward a local landmark or racing down the 140-foot waterslide into a refreshing pool, the resort's offerings cover the complete spectrum of leisure and exploration.

Each evening, the California-quality sunset is complemented by the soft sound of crystal singing bowls, an ancient ritual known for healing and relaxation through sound and vibration. It is hard to believe that a setting like this, so sensitively woven into the breathtaking natural landscape, is real and located just a few minutes south of Los Angeles, but perhaps you'd better drop by just to be sure.

A gracious, Old World ambience permeates the resort's 102 acres, from the guest rooms, suites, bungalows, casitas, and villas to the abundant gardens, courtyards, and terraces. One couple chose a Mediterranean-tiled staircase facing Catalina Point as the location for their post-nuptial sword ceremony and then headed to the Marineland ballroom for dinner and dancing.

Photograph by Joe Buissink

Photograph by Boutwell Studio

Indoors and out, practically every space in the resort could serve as a special event venue. The property has played host to Hollywood films, television shows, and outdoor concerts. Formal occasions are generally hosted in one of our three main ballrooms: the 18,000-square-foot Palos Verdes grand ballroom and terrace with adjacent pre-function spaces, the 6,600-square-foot Marineland ballroom, or the more intimate 4,400-square-foot Catalina room and terrace with endless ocean views of Catalina Island. All of the venues seamlessly intertwine nature within the space.

Photograph courtesy of Terranea Resort

"You know there is something magical about the design of a venue when it can have a corporate seminar on one side of the property, and on the other side the romantic couple on a balcony is none the wiser."

—Julie Sevilla

Photograph by Aaron Delesie

Photograph by Aaron Delesie

Photograph by Boutwell Studio

Photograph by Joe Buissink

Photograph by Joe Buissink

"Radiant ocean views and architecture with a seamless indoor-outdoor connection define the classic California lifestyle experience."

—Tracy Koven

Carolyn Chen, chief entertaining officer of The Special Day, plans many of the weddings held here, and oceanfront ceremonies have become a Terranea signature since the scenery is so exquisite. To complement the views, we have fantastic dining options for both event guests and vacationers. Mar'sel, Spanish for "sea" and French for "salt," is the epitome of Southern California cuisine, featuring homegrown vegetables and herbs. All seven of our oceanview dining venues promise to surprise and delight.

Photograph by Aaron Delesie

views

A place's sense of history goes a long way in establishing the character of an event. Terranea's aesthetic was inspired by the rich history of Spanish explorers who first discovered the Southern California coastline in the 1500s, and the resort's very name reflects the Mediterranean nature of its coastal setting.

HOUSE OF AN

CATHERINE AN

Soon after the An family opened its celebrated Crustacean restaurants—first in San Francisco and then in Beverly Hills—enthusiastic California foodies began clamoring for a venue where they could host events while serving their guests Chef Helene An's famous blend of Vietnamese, Chinese, and French cuisine. What they got was not one but two venues, each with a distinct look and feel but still with the traditional hospitality and cutting-edge presentation An family devotees have come to love.

AnQi, which opened in Orange County in 2009, is a sleek, sexy restaurant that features private rooms ideal for hosting events. A bold fashion runway cuts through the center of the main space, doubling as an elevated dining platform. The newest addition and brainchild of Catherine An is Tiato, a market garden café located in Santa Monica. Named after her mother's favorite herb, an ingredient known for its rich health benefits and exciting flavor, Tiato is a gourmet eatery and retail market that offers fresh bites on the go, and a wine, beer, and Asian tapas bar in addition to an ideal event space. Tiato also serves as an example of the An family's dedication to earth-friendly practices. The majority of the venue was built with reclaimed wood, and recycled tiles, eco-fabrics, and recycled glass platters figure into the space's eco-conscious design. The fresh herb and citrus garden patio provides ingredients—including, of course, tiato—for Helene's famously fresh and healthy dishes.

We do everything we can to be as green as possible—it's always been a big priority. Besides growing some of our own produce, we try to compost after every event and choose materials and supplies based on how earth-friendly they are.

Photograph by Mario Sanchez

Photograph by Alex Vasilescu

Photograph by Alex Vasilescu

Photograph by Alex Vasilescu

Photograph by Alex Vasilescu

"Californians care about their health and environment, an attitude that completely matches our philosophy."
—Catherine An

Our clients enjoy working with us because we offer a wide variety of venue options, each with its own wow factor, and when you pair that with Mama's cuisine an unforgettable event experience is inevitable.

Photograph by Jessica Boone

views

When we set out to build Tiato, the existing space naturally lent itself to being very organic. A complete overhaul of the interior was necessary, but the building's great bone structure made it very easy to integrate sustainable materials and eco-friendly design. While it's a very versatile venue, the earthy yet chic atmosphere doesn't require a lot of decoration.

KORAKIA

PAULETTE MONARREZ

The flickering lanterns, lush tropical landscapes, and bougainvillea-scented air are deceiving—what could easily be mistaken for sultry Tangier or the sun-drenched Mediterranean is in fact Palm Springs, location of the hotel that both *Forbes* and *The New York Times* named one of the sexiest in the world. Korakia embraces its artistic, eclectic history, continuing on in the Continental style in which it was first built in 1924. Serving as the getaway for Scottish painter Gordon Coutts, the villa known as Dar Marroc recaptured the essence of the Moroccan architecture and lifestyle Coutts grew up with. Famous artists and celebrities would stop by to visit the painter, enjoying the property's blend of Southern European charm and North African accents.

After falling into disrepair, the villa was rescued in 1989 and joined by its neighbor to create Korakia, a Mediterranean-style pensione with a name that means "crow" in Greek. Guests now arrive through the distinctive keyhole-shaped entrance and heavy Moorish wooden doors before finding themselves in an exotic oasis of vivid earth-tone hues, stone waterfalls, and groves of citrus trees. The bungalows, guesthouses, gardens, and pools have provided breathtaking backdrops for some of the world's best photographers and graced the pages of *Condé Nast Traveler, Vogue, Marie Claire*, and *Architectural Digest*. True to its history, Korakia remains a popular rendezvous for the artistic crowd, including renowned actors, writers, and producers looking for an enchanting escape.

Our close proximity to the San Jacinto Mountains gives the whole property a rustic aura, something we really showcase in the architecture and landscaping. From the torch-lit swimming pools to the outdoor yoga, we really encourage our guests to spend as much time outside as possible.

Photograph by John Solano Photography

Photograph by John Solano Photography

Photograph by John Solano Photography

Photograph by John Solano Photography

"Natural settings lend themselves to as much or as little decoration as you wish."

—Paulette Monarrez

Events at Korakia have a magical feel to them. There's something so romantic and intimate about the resort to begin with that hosting a wedding only magnifies those feelings. The unique surroundings are also ideal for a think-tank getaway or inspirational meeting— nothing clears your head better than communing with nature.

Photograph by John Solano Photography

views

A lot of hotels focus on technology: flat-screen television sets, wireless internet, iPod docks. We go a different route, offering bocce ball, complimentary bicycles, and classic film screenings alfresco. Vacations, no matter the length, should be an escape from reality, a chance to connect with your family, friends, and even yourself. Unplug every once in a while and take time to enjoy your surroundings.

r.s.v.p.

directions

celebrate

The festivities continue in honor of...

Julian

the Details

MARC FRIEDLAND/CREATIVE INTELLIGENCE, INC.

MARC FRIEDLAND

The first thing most people notice about Marc Friedland is that he does things a little differently. The second thing they notice is that he does them better. Rather than just create invitations that deliver the who, what, why, and where, he focuses on delivering the "wow." Marc and his team at Creative Intelligence have been turning out eye-catching, imaginative, elegant, and sometimes downright wacky invitations since 1986, even writing the definitive book on the subject, *Invitations by Marc Friedland*. Going way beyond the expected is the company's specialty, and its focus has since transformed to fuse genius marketing strategy, cutting-edge creativity, and impeccable style into an integrated, comprehensive, graphic communications experience.

An experiential branding agency renowned for its ability to evolve events into experiences through design—what exactly does that mean? It means that non-profit organizations, corporations, and individuals often take their décor and theme cues from Marc's design and branding insights. His first impressions, whether conveying sophistication for a graceful dinner party or building excitement for an exotic weekend getaway, communicate and express the emotions that set the tone for the event to come. The tactile experience is a must—feathers, silks, crystal, wood, and even Astroturf can accompany his work. Whatever best expresses the heart and soul of the celebration finds its way into Marc's studio, where it is then designed and assembled to pack a multi-sensory punch. Over the years, Marc estimates that he's invited over 2 million people to well over 4,500 events, some of the most significant global celebrations and commemorations of the century.

We've been doing the iconic invitations for the annual event Simply Shakespeare for over 20 years, and while the construction remains the same, the theme is constantly evolving. We always find a way to make the designs irreverent but still appropriate—we push the envelope, if you will, promising an evening that's truly "Bard none." The 2009 invite was a reflection of the show's superhero theme.

Photograph by John Ellis

Photograph by John Ellis

Photograph by Gia Canali

Photograph by Gia Canali

Paul Allen, co-founder of Microsoft, invited 400 colleagues and friends on a four-day trip to Russia, and what better way to prepare his guests for the opulence and richness of the excursion than with engraved, imported Fabergé eggs, a cherrywood box overflowing with satin and brocade, and a custom-designed imperial crest? One guest was so excited to receive his invitation he brought it on "The Late Show with David Letterman" just to show it off.

As you all know, this past winter came our marri
What comes next is Mommy & Me and long strolls with a baby car
We've kept the stork busy, flying about.
To discover our secret, crack the egg and find out!
...ere's a party in store if you really must know.
It's a baby shower, and we'd love you to go!

Linda & Steve

The thrill of interactive discovery is at the heart of all of our work. What many forget is that invitations should actually be "inviting" and engage guests from the very start. Inside the hand-delivered polka dot and silk-covered boxes was a single hand-painted ostrich egg and a limerick encouraging recipients to crack their egg to find the baby shower details. It was witty and hip with a dash of whimsy, and the invitation directly inspired the feel of the actual event, designed by Shay Watson of Aesthetica Events.

Photograph by John Ellis

Photograph by Dave Schwep

Photograph by Dave Schwep

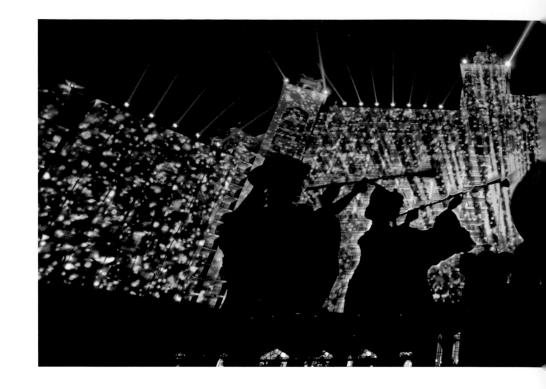

Photograph by John Ellis

Photograph by John Ellis

"Capturing and communicating the true essence of an event's vibe requires the passion of Picasso, the playfulness of Willy Wonka, the insight of Freud, and the style and grace of Coco Chanel."

—Marc Friedland

The opening of Atlantis, The Palm, a magnificent resort on manmade island The Palm Jumeirah in Dubai, was the birth of an architectural icon and naturally called for an equally grand invitation. Hand-crafted gold and crystal miniatures of the new resort, surrounded by such landmarks as the Eiffel Tower, Sydney Opera House, and Taj Mahal, were nestled in an incredibly detailed taffeta-lined box before being hand-delivered to 2,500 guests around the world.

Photograph courtesy of Kerzner International

Photograph by John Ellis

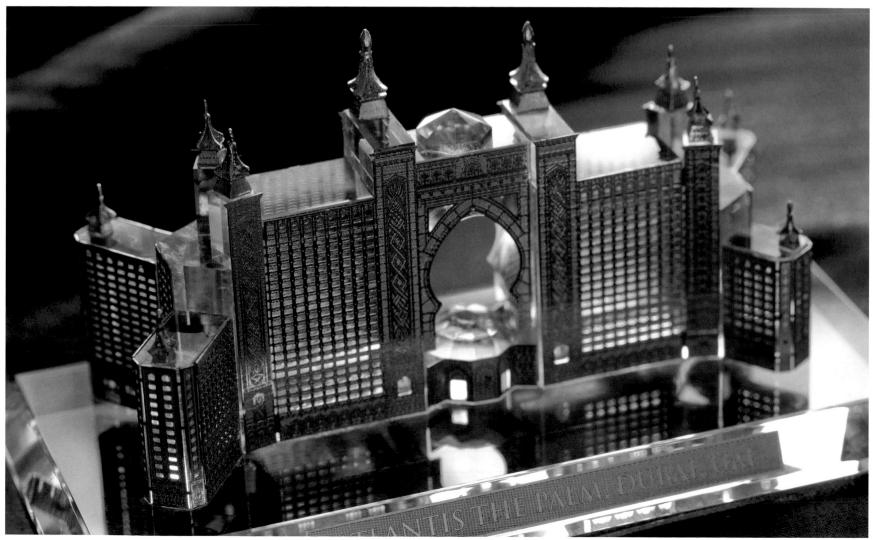

Photograph by John Ellis

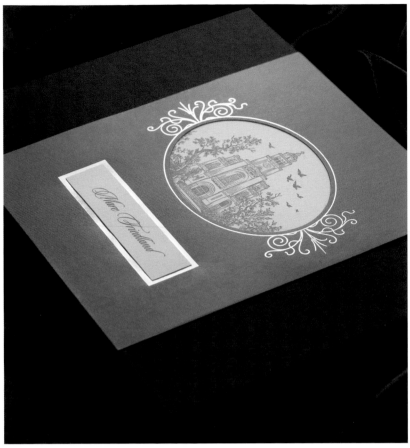

EÓN
HIJOS

Photograph by John Ellis

Besides using such gorgeous materials as eggplant and olive green taffeta, gold leaf, and toile to convey the picturesque setting of the bride's childhood Dominican Republic church, we included a custom-engraved antique bronze taleidoscope to symbolize the beautiful facets of light and love, captured in the couple's adventures in romance.

Photograph by John Ellis

Photograph by John Ellis

Photograph by John Ellis

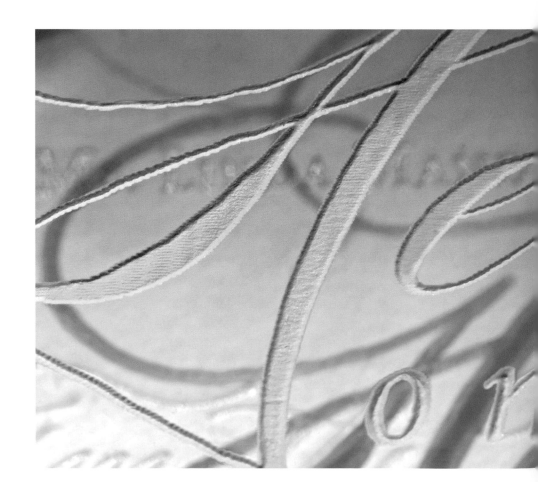

Photograph by John Ellis

Photograph by John Ellis

Noted music producer Timbaland's wedding in Aruba was, quite literally, "Heaven on Earth," so we designed his invitation accordingly. A personalized Lucite box for each guest contained hundreds of white feathers and a sole baby blue feather, symbolizing the couple's singular love for each other. Etched, engraved, and embossed, the boxes and accompanying shantung silk bags were personalized for each guest.

Photograph by John Ellis

Photograph by Joe Atlas

Photograph by John Ellis

Photograph by Joe Atlas

Photograph by John Ellis

"Invitations need to be inviting, not just convey information."

—Marc Friedland

We are definitely not afraid to use color, nor are we afraid of three-dimensional objects. Invitations shouldn't be categorized as simply ink on paper, but as little works of art—mixed-media masterpieces that engage the recipient, whet his or her appetite, and serve as heartfelt keepsakes long after the dessert is served. Whether embroidered raw silk bento boxes or pop-up retro television sets, the goal is always to make an impactful first impression and leave a lasting memory of the experience of the event. All photos styled by Sunday Henrickson.

Photograph by Gia Canali

views

The first thing an invitation should do is establish anticipation of the event. This is the beginning of the relationship between the giver and the receiver and it should convey how delighted the hosts are to include the guest in sharing the momentous experience. Making keepsakes and items that people will treasure for years to come is an extension of that relationship and a true celebration of love and life. Connecting, communicating, and celebrating is what we've been doing best for nearly 25 years.

Laura Hooper Calligraphy

LAURA HOOPER

In an age where invitations are increasingly created via do-it-yourself kits and laser printers, or done away with entirely in favor of internet messages, it's refreshing to know there is still at least one woman who practices the classically beautiful art form of calligraphy. Laura Hooper has been entranced with the delicate, swooping strokes ever since she picked up a pen at age 12, but it wasn't until college that she realized her hobby might make sense as a viable business. After penning the envelopes for a friend's wedding, word of mouth spread, and soon Laura was able to put her business degree to good use with the opening of Laura Hooper Calligraphy in 2002.

Since then, Laura's hand-lettered invitations, save-the-dates, collection of reception items, and whimsically personalized maps have been putting a modern twist on tradition while delighting scores of high-profile hosts. Popular online stationer Minted.com doubled Laura's exposure by securing her as one of its calligraphers shortly after it launched.

Laura's couture line, Lucky Orchid Invitations, combines her love of the refined with eco-conscious, 100-percent cotton paper and soy ink, a green trend that's gaining in popularity. With over 20 different lettering varieties available, ranging from elaborate curlicues to streamlined script, there's something for every host's taste and style. Ecstatic guests often inform their hosts that even the envelopes have remained on the refrigerator long after arriving, instead of joining other, less exquisite envelopes in the trash bin. Do-it-yourself kits, be afraid.

Sunny, fresh, and effortlessly elegant, the Summer Garden letterpress design pairs canary yellow with navy blue, while buoyant script conveys the joy of the occasion.

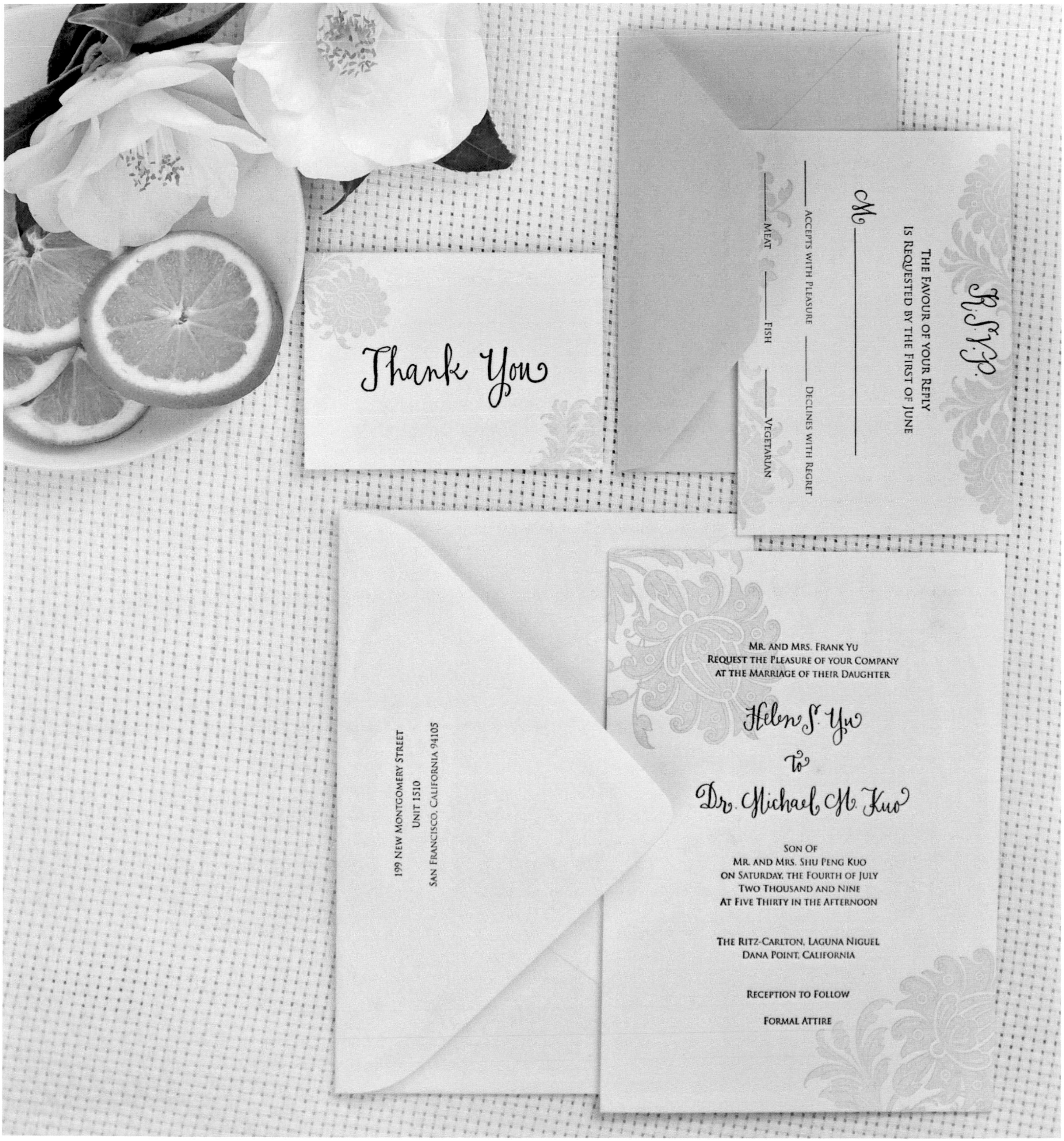
R.S.V.P.
The Favour of your Reply
Is Requested by the First of June
M
Accepts with Pleasure
Declines with Regret
Meat
Fish
Vegetarian
Thank You
199 New Montgomery Street
Unit 1510
San Francisco, California 94105
Mr. and Mrs. Frank Yu
Request the Pleasure of your Company
at the Marriage of their Daughter
Helen S. Yu
to
Dr. Michael M. Kuo
Son Of
Mr. and Mrs. Shu Peng Kuo
on Saturday, the Fourth of July
Two Thousand and Nine
At Five Thirty in the Afternoon
The Ritz-Carlton, Laguna Niguel
Dana Point, California
Reception to Follow
Formal Attire

Photograph by Steve Steinhardt Photography

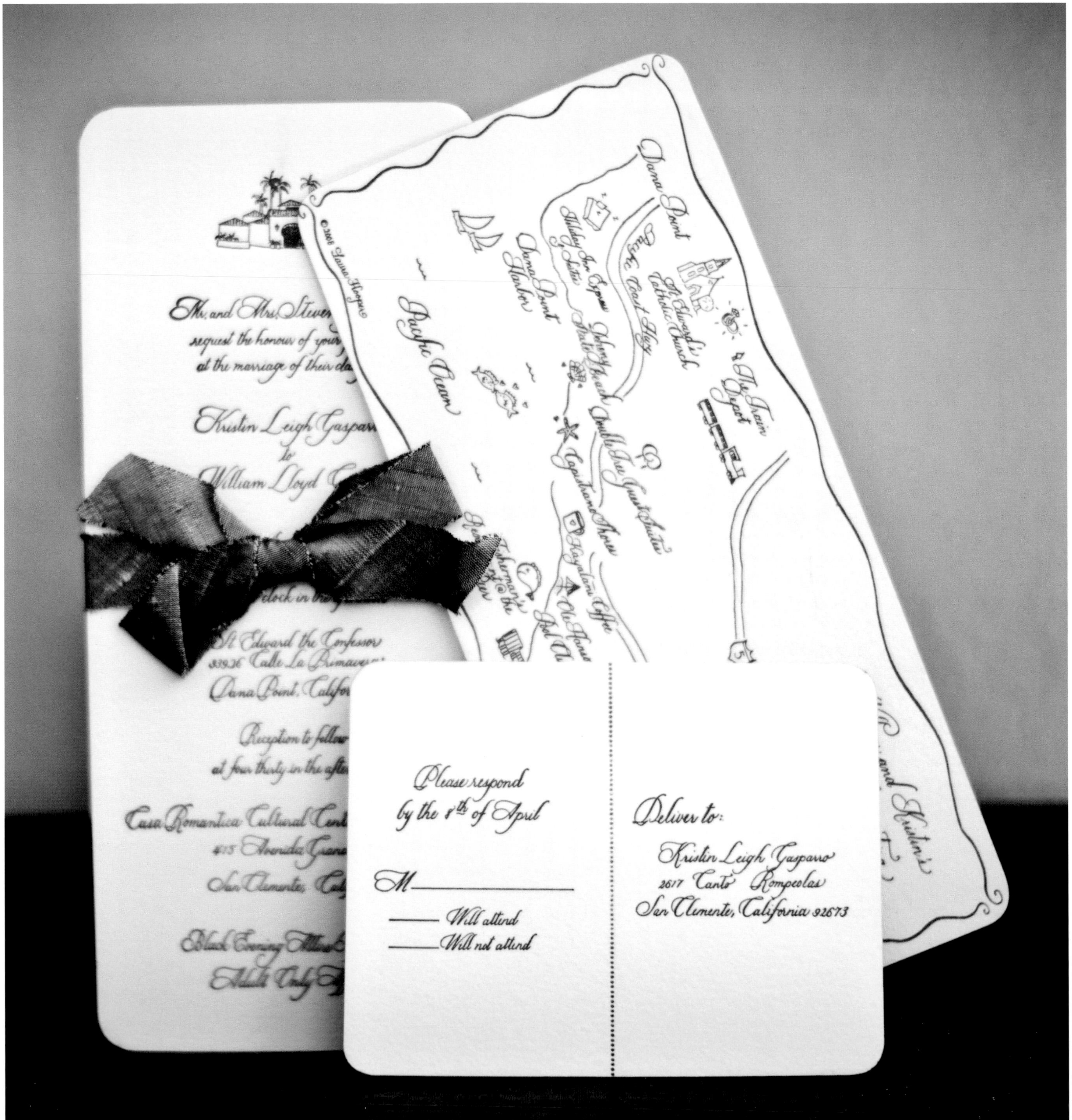

Photograph by Mi Belle Photography

Photograph by Steve Steinhardt Photography

Photograph by Steve Steinhardt Photography

Above: Some designs, like the Venice, are popular because they don't mimic a specific floral design. Others might rely less on a graphic and concentrate instead on colors that match their theme or location. Seafoam green and taupe echoed a ceremony in Laguna Beach without being overtly nautical.

Facing page: The graceful lettering, regal antique gold and pewter colors, and silk dupioni bow are all reminiscent of a formal invitation, but two important touches kept the set from being stuffy: the map and its sheer size. Printed on thick paper cotton, the invitation was letter size, much bigger than the traditional 5x7. The couple was married in Orange County and I drew their beautiful venue at the top for a fanciful touch.

"Calligraphy isn't an archaic art form; it adds a personal touch that's impossible to replicate."

—Laura Hooper

Photograph by Lisa Franchot Photography

Photograph by Mi Belle Photography

Photograph by Mi Belle Photography

"It's really important that the design reflects your own individuality; after all, that's why you chose to go custom!"

—Laura Hooper

Right: The menu card not only incorporated the couple's colors of ivory, soft beige, and navy blue, but writing the names in a very pale gold across the band added a bit of pop without being overpowering.

Facing page: Calligraphy doesn't have to be limited to only paper; we can apply the designs to everything from sand dollars to tote bags. Sometimes I'll give a tote as a sample, and the host will use it to carry their event materials around while visiting vendors and locations. The positive response I get back from situations like that is unbelievable.

Photograph by Steve Steinhardt Photography

views

I like to ask hosts to bring me color swatches and clippings that inspire them. If I'm doing a wedding set for them, the clippings don't even have to be wedding-based, just anything that reflects their personalities, interests, likes, and hobbies. By taking a look at them outside of the world of event planning, I can better understand what might work best for them.

ROCK PAPER SCISSORS DESIGN

RACHEL BAKER

At first glance, it's easy to mistake an invitation from Rock Paper Scissors Design as a luxury gift. A silk box adorned with ribbons or a wood carton ornamented with feathers would certainly rival a coveted package from any posh boutique. But what lies inside—the request for family and friends to join in a celebration—is more precious than any trinket. That is what makes Rachel Baker's job so gratifying; a job, Rachel says, she didn't initially intend to have.

After studying advertising at the Art Center College of Design in Pasadena, Rachel envisioned herself joining a high-powered ad agency in New York or Los Angeles. Settling briefly in the deserts of New Mexico while her Air Force husband attended dental school did not fit the plan, but it was that solitary existence that pushed Rachel to turn a hobby into a career. Since 2004, Rachel has been a one-woman whirlwind, designing and producing distinctive invitations, menus, placecards, programs, thank you notes, and even wine labels. Her creations range from delicately elegant to extraordinarily funky, but always with a touch of the unexpected.

Be it paper, metal, acrylic, or cloth, Rachel uses only the finest materials and most skilled craftsmen to construct her products. Tremendous attention to detail and her highly personalized approach ensures that recipients are continually astounded. Little surprises, like a s'mores kit for a Lake Placid wedding or printed wine corks for save-the-dates, show how Rock Paper Scissors Design is always thinking in and out of the box.

For an outdoor wedding in Atlanta, I had to convey rustic elegance with a heavy dose of Southern charm. Along with the colorful tablecloths from Wildflower Linens, a magenta silk box with a rhinestone embellishment and letterpress printing made a statement, but what really blew everyone away was that the invitation was actually printed wood.

TOGETHER WITH THEIR FAMILIES
Erika Meneke Bates
AND
Mayce Edward Christopher Webber III
INVITE YOU TO JOIN THEM
AS THEY EXCHANGE THE VOWS OF MARRIAGE
SUNDAY, THE SIXTH DAY OF SEPTEMBER
TWO THOUSAND AND NINE
AT HALF PAST FOUR O'CLOCK IN THE AFTERNOON
THE WEBBER FARM
TYRONE, GEORGIA
RECEPTION FOLLOWING THE CEREMONY

KINDLY RESPOND BY THE

M

ACCE

Itinerary

Photograph by Laura Grier, Beautiful Day Photography

You are cordially invited
to join us in celebrating
the 50th wedding anniversary of

Mr. & Mrs. Delmar Schmidt

Saturday, the fourteenth day of November
Two thousand and nine
at six o'clock in the evening
the Viceroy
Palm Springs, California

Black Tie

Please RSVP by November fifth
annies08@gmail.com

Photograph by Laura Grier, Beautiful Day Photography

Photograph by Chet Williams Photography

We invite you to join us a

Sunshine De

and

Christopher L

Photograph by Chet Williams Photography

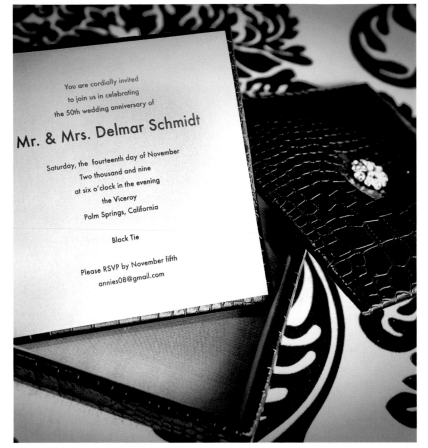

ST...MARIA IS TURNING 21

A NOT-SO-SLEEPOVER ON THE EVE OF MARIA'S 21ST

TRIKES MIDNIGHT, WE ARE GOING TO PAINT THE TOWN

AND GIVE HER 21 SURPRISES

SATURDAY NIGHT 6/11/08

N COCKTAILS AT TEN O'CLOCK

E AT 12 FROM KILEY'S HOUSE, IN A LIMO

RL FUN AND THE REAL DRINKS WILL BEGIN

FACE MASK, I.D., A FANCY DRE

ANGEL ON YOUR S

Photograph by Chet Williams Photography

"An invitation is the guest's first impression of an event."

—Rachel Baker

Right: Course after delectable course was fire-branded directly onto the wooden menu card. A twist of copper wire, natural stone, and a small bud brought nature to the tables, which were dressed in cloths from Wildflower Linen

Facing page top left: Faux crocodile, etched metal, and graphic fabric from Wildflower Linen equals modern sophistication for a 50th wedding anniversary.

Facing page top right: Designing tropical elegance with a fall color palette might seem like a challenge at first, but orchids come in a rainbow of color choices. Selecting just the right silk bloom to go with hand-starched burlap and emerald rhinestone accents was easier than anticipated.

Facing page bottom left: With the eco-chic movement gaining momentum, options such as plant-based ink and seeded paper that guests can take home and plant are becoming more popular.

Facing page bottom right: A 21st birthday party was the perfect opportunity to show off grown-up style on girlie pink metallic paper.

Photograph by Paul Barnett

views

When you plan a destination wedding, it's a given that a large number of invited guests won't or can't make the trip. But I've had instances where the invitation was so intriguing that every single person on the guest list showed up for the wedding. Now that's exciting!

SEQUOIA PRODUCTIONS
CHERYL CECCHETTO

Cheryl Cecchetto and her eclectic team at Sequoia Productions, each an accomplished artist in their own right, have dedicated themselves to discovering innovative ways to erase that thin line between dreamscape and reality. Chasing creative rainbows has always been the guiding light for Sequoia's unique design ideas, and driven by Cheryl's nova-like energy and the enthusiasm of her creative team, it's easy to see why the company is a longstanding favorite for hosts seeking high-end events dripping with feeling and originality.

Still, the grand end of design and execution is only half the quotient for success. According to Cheryl, it's the experience Sequoia strives to create, not the event. An enjoyable experience is a memorable one, with the memories giving the event its life beyond the "last call." But if memories are the life of the party, then interpersonal relationships are the soul. Sequoia forges personal relationships with its hosts and vendors as a matter of necessity rather than protocol. Something Olivia Yu, Sequoia's creative communication director, has discovered is that having a host who's as excited about their contribution to the collaboration process is instrumental in the quest to deliver a personalized affair. This she terms "graph-onality," a concept Olivia knows better than most. Well-designed invitations, seating cards, menus, and other materials become imbued with the hosts' personalities, sharing with the guest insights into their life, their joys, their interests. You could say graphic design is yet another tool Sequoia uses to express the art of celebration.

Surprise! An invitation for a surprise birthday party should be innovative and fun, so we mailed the invitation itself as a surprise package to the guest. The invitation should always be an extension of the event, and therefore, always entertaining. When it comes to invitations, think fun first, practical second.

Photograph by ShaneSoto.com

Photograph by ShaneSoto.com

AK
PASSENGER TICKET & BAGGAGE CHECK

SAT 02FEB 2008   6:30PM
TIME

AK13   FIRST
FLIGHT   CLASS

13A
SEAT

DIRECT FLIGHT
STATUS

BAR MITZVAH

SANTA MONICA
02 FEB 2008
DEPART
CALIFORNIA

AK
PASSPORT

AK
AIRLINES

BOARDING P

NAME OF PASSENGER

GATE NO.

13
FLIGHT NO.   02FEB
DATE

AK AIRLINES
CARRIER

>>> NON-REFUNDABLE

Photograph by ShaneSoto.com

WONDER WOMAN IS TURNING 50!

C & R / MENU

| FIRST COURSE |

SALAD TRIO FEATURING

OOM TOMATO WITH

MOZZARELLA

Photograph by ZenTodd.com

Photograph by ShaneSoto.com

"If the event is the marriage between guest and celebration, the invitation is the first kiss."

—Olivia Yu

Right: The theatrical spotlight highlighting the guest of honor's name ties in his interest for theater. An honoree's interests can be an insightful clue into their personality, making a guest feel at once privileged and curious. That's the purpose of the invite. always leave the guest wanting more.

Facing page top left: The use of deep colors, embossed foil, and fabric on a gala fundraiser invitation add dimension and texture, which in turn builds anticipation.

Facing page top right: A young man's passion for flying was fulfilled at the Spitfire Grill Aviation Restaurant. Table seating cards resembling boarding passes bore his initials, replacing those of an airline.

Facing page bottom left: A quaint dinner menu in soft tones with a delicate Asian influence honors the couple's request for a clean, open, and simple motif.

Facing page bottom right: The guest of honor and her vivacious "super" personality inspired the eye-popping colors and iconic figure of Wonder Woman. Even small details like the riveted binding and stamp on the envelope help carry the theme.

Photograph by ShaneSoto.com

views

When it comes to designing elements such as invitations, seating cards, menus etc., it's important to note that the eye is the doorway to the soul. The communion of aesthetics and pleasure is first experienced through one's sense of sight, therefore choose attractive, emotional colors and textures. Also, know what emotion you are trying to convey, whether it's joy, excitement, zaniness, or maybe something more subtle and moving. The text is simply for information; it's the "emotion" behind the text that the guest will remember.

SOOLIP PAPERIE & PRESS
WANDA WEN

The digital age affects everyday life, allowing an unparalleled efficiency and convenience; yet technology has left people starving for tactile elements and for something worthy of pausing and taking notice. Enter Soolip Paperie & Press. Founded nearly two decades ago by Wanda Wen, whose affinity for the paper arts goes back to childhood Valentine's Day cards, her collection has expanded from a hobby of accumulating paper scraps for her own repurposing to a full-time profession in paper art that fulfills her creative spirit and her passion for satisfying other people's visions.

Based on the idea of bringing out the beauty in the simple things, Soolip's treasures embrace nature and life's common objects. By implementing and portraying them in the most delightful ways, such as thin, silver twine wrapped around placecards or delicately pressed sage leaves to ornament an invitation, ordinary items transform into distinguished features.

The signature tone of Soolip's designs is derived from its focus on handmade items and letterpress printing. With the extra time and care put into the end result, guests sense an inherent quality of thoughtfulness and translate it into a feeling of warmth and importance. From the highly decorative patterns of Japanese yuzen silk screens to the natural fiber inclusions of Thai Unryus, from the one-dimensional refined invitation to the luxurious, multi-piece package, Soolip's creations become works of art.

From a young age, recycling and reusing what others considered waste was important to me. I felt that an awareness and respect for the earth, which sustains us, was achievable, even in everyday moments. One way we embody a green mentality is through our tree-free gift wrap paper, which is made from recycled cotton material from India.

Photograph by Jules Bianchi

Photograph by Jules Bianchi

Together in love

Summer Anne Hadl

and

Mark Anthony Mel

invite you to celebrate their

Sunday, the fourth of A

Two thousand seve

Photograph by Jules Bianchi

Photograph by Jules Bianchi

"Events are successful when guests feel special, honored, and considered—paper elements are an important, tactile part of the process in creating enduring memories."

—Wanda Wen

Right: Aleksey Shirokov, who was formally trained in classic European calligraphy and once worked as a calligrapher for the Russian government, is a talented team member who adds a unique touch to our distinct designs.

Facing page top: To help a luxury automaker promote its new vehicle to dealerships, we created a living presentation. Beautifully wrapped in a champagne hue, the box reveals crushed glass, LED lights, fresh succulents, and a hand-bound, letterpress notebook filled with the how-to's of a fabulous launch party.

Facing page bottom: Elements of nature, such as real dried, pressed daisies or vintage glass berries, are perfect adornments to any project and reflect poignant attention to detail.

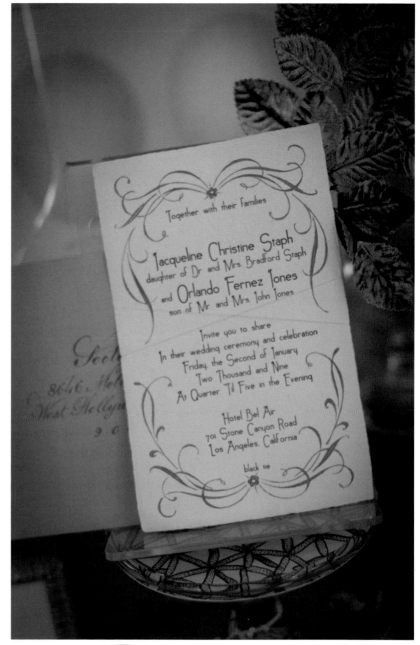

Photograph by Alyssa Nicol

views

Remember to always see the beauty in simplicity. Don't overdo things. Allow the wonder of nature or the inherent qualities of the elements to speak for themselves.

Creating an

Ambience

R. Jack Balthazar

NIKI DELACUEVA | RENE DELACUEVA

When Rene and Niki Delacueva say they love to throw parties, they're not kidding. They are so into entertaining friends and hosting fabulous soirées that in 2001 they decided to make a career of it, despite the fact they possessed no formal training. Niki, a former orthopedic researcher, and Rene, who has a degree in finance, began running their company out of their tiny garage. Now headquartered in Pasadena with multiple production and warehouse facilities, they have the pleasure of being one of the most sought-after event design firms in the country.

They explain their company's name—R. Jack Balthazar—as the moniker of their firstborn son. As of now, daughter Mila Jack is their only offspring, but endearing quirks such as this are a hallmark of Niki and Rene's style. They strive to take the stuffiness out of high-profile events by creating environments that engage the senses and put people at ease. They believe that guests find comfort in what they know, and so they try to achieve a space where a guest can enter and gravitate immediately toward something familiar. Once guests have reached that sense of belonging, the Delacuevas push the envelope and give them a visual experience that surpasses their reality.

Also serious travel buffs, the couple brings a first-hand experience of different cultures and lifestyles to the design and architecture of their events. Ever the zealous collectors, they've been known to plan their journeys based on the shopping—the flea markets outside Paris, the night markets in Bangkok, and the handicraft markets in Jaipur.

Inspiration came from the exotica of Old World seaports: gypsy seafarers traveling the world on tall mast-ships. We created an outdoor village setting with a mixture of seating options and collected elements. The tabletop décor was seaport-market inspired, utilizing market fresh flowers and herbs as the focus, with nautical knots, weathered metals, woven baskets and orbs, birdcages and vintage glass chandeliers, compasses and clocks, sea glass floats and jugs completing the look. We spent months collecting vintage lanterns and textiles for tent draping, floor pillows, and area rugs, giving it an eclectic, aged atmosphere.

Photograph by Niki Delacueva

Photograph by Laura Kleinhenz/Docuvitae

Photograph by Niki Delacueva

Photograph by Aaron Delesie

Above: To further the nomadic, global vibe, we created different types of floral and non-floral décor for the varied height and differently shaped tables, incorporating the elements of air, water, land, and sky.

Above right: Often the challenge with a spectacular ocean view is how to add personality to the space without trying to compete with the scenery. For this wedding ceremony, we used backless benches to keep the overall seating profile low and accented them with woven fans decorated with floral blooms. A woven runner and dark bowls of floating orchids and palm leaves created a lush, vibrant island feel.

Facing page: The dinner was a showcase for a new tequila maker and the brand's approach to pair tequila with Asian dinner fare. We wanted the tabletop and environment to exude both cultural nuances, so wrought-iron candelabras and Mexican pottery were paired with Japanese bento box-inspired lanterns and red coral.

"Special events shouldn't be about fantasy or ostentation; they should focus on creating experiential environments."

—Rene Delacueva

Photograph by Simone & Martin Photography

Photograph by Niki Delacueva

Photograph by Niki Delacueva

Photograph by Niki Delacueva

Top: When we drape ballrooms, they often become void of any architectural details. To further the event's residential vibe, we added luxurious banquette sofas and upholstered slipper chairs—a refined mixture of table shapes and sizes, each with a different tablescape design. Cozy lounge vignettes were placed around the space, offering guests an alternative area to mingle and celebrate.

Bottom: For the birthday of a very special client, we transformed a sushi restaurant into a hip and chic party space that mixed Asian elements with bold graphic accents. Suspended behind a lounge vignette of glamorous leather and sparkly pillows were art pieces composed of green cymbidium orchids, green roses, and green spider mums in a circular graphic matching the invites. Guests sat on black velvet ottomans at low wood tables, while organza fabric created a kabuki effect and helped to define spaces in the restaurant.

Facing page top: What is amazing about the dinner setting is that it takes place on a patch of lawn in between two buildings at a hotel in Palm Springs. The hosts wanted to bring a vintage supper club vibe to an open-air setting, and since what we all envisioned did not exist we created the environment from the ground up.

Facing page bottom: While many hosts tend to shy away from hotel ballrooms, they are ideal in certain situations because we can control the entire environment: We don't have to worry about the weather, we can control the lighting, and there are a myriad of built-in rigging options. The drawback is that oftentimes the existing walls and carpet do not match the envisioned event décor. To start with a clean slate, we carpeted the entire ballroom and draped the perimeter in diaphanous champagne fabric.

Previous pages: We wanted this room to have the feeling of an intimate dinner at home, but we didn't want to have one long table for seating. Instead, we opted for smaller round tables seating fewer guests than traditional larger banquet rounds, to not only fill the space but also create intimate seating vignettes. The layers of washed brocade and Irish linen tablecloths added a residential sensibility while hundreds of pillar candles adorned the centers of the tables, giving the impression the entire room was lit by candlelight. Towering columns of vines and greens with white garden roses and hanging lanterns created visual interest along the perimeter of the celebration, softening the lines of the original brick walls.

Photograph by Niki Delacueva

Photograph by Niki Delacueva

Above: Whenever we need a pop of color, we love to use shades of orange; it's bold enough to be fun and inviting but it's not overly feminine or "wedding-y"—not to mention it looks warm and beautiful under candlelight. We kept the tables dark with chocolate brown linens and bouquets of lush orchids in shades of citrus, but depth was added to the space by uplighting the surrounding hedges.

Left: Mokara and cymbidium orchids, gloriosa lilies, garden roses, and hydrangeas in vibrant shades of fuchsia, chartreuse, and citrus created a vivid, verdant garden down the entire table. Wrought-iron candelabras with pillar candles complemented the Moorish feeling of the space.

Facing page: For a wedding ceremony set in the grand lobby of the Hollywood Roosevelt Hotel, we relied on lighting and a mass of candlelight to give the illusion that the space was somehow magically illuminated by moonlight.

Photograph by Akiko Photo

Photograph by Jose Mandojana/Docuvitae

Photograph by Stephanie Hogue

Photograph by Stephanie Hogue

Photograph by Niki Delacueva

"For one evening, our clients get to provide to their guests a glimpse into their 'vision,' and we help to articulate that vision."

—Niki Delacueva

Right: After draping the walls and carpeting the floor of this storied hotel ballroom, we added our own luxurious touches, including oversized gilded wall mirrors and upholstered chairs and sofas intermixed with traditional ballroom chairs for guest seating.

Facing page top: We wanted a very neutral color palette but with a bold pop. Deep red roses with pink cymbidium orchids provided jolts of color on the tabletops. Pearlized capiz shell chandeliers and curtains added layers of personality and luxury to the outdoor dining canopies. Capiz shell discs also adorned upholstered vases and served as a graphic yet refined napkin detail.

Facing page bottom: For an intimate tastemaker's dinner in the Hollywood Hills, we dressed the table in graphic linen and created floralscapes in shades of white, playing off of the textures of the white florals.

Photograph by Niki Delacueva

views

One of the most important variables in event décor is the host's chemistry and connection with their designer. We spend a lot of time getting to know our potential hosts, gaining an understanding of how they live and how they want to entertain. For us, inspiration comes from the product we are showcasing, the artist that is being promoted, or the radiant bride and how she wants to be seen on her most important day. Our most memorable events are those where our clients trusted us to articulate their style, their story, and their vision.

ED LIBBY & COMPANY INC.

ED LIBBY

If you think "straight off the runway" is only associated with clothing and accessories, then you haven't been to an Ed Libby event. Ed Libby & Company was the first design studio to use layers of ingredients to blend atmosphere with living art to create a dramatic new dimension. Floral design and event production will never be the same.

Decreed the "darling designer of New York society," Ed keeps challenging himself to reinvent—inspired by his clients, a love of travel, and artistic talent. His diverse designs serve both to support his success and to distinctly represent each client's personality. But he wouldn't have it any other way: Challenge is what unearths creative brilliance. After 25 years of designing celebrated events from coast-to-coast and abroad, Ed leaves nothing to chance. Amidst his stunning backgrounds, accuracy counts. Each event's interior has been immaculately sketched down to the last crucial detail for the host—even the napkin rings go through painstaking selection. When the time for the event comes, the stage is strategically set for glamorous hostesses to enjoy their evening among "vignettes of visual delight."

Whether an Ed Libby-designed event is a glamorous society soirée or an outrageous celebrity birthday party, guests are struck by his chameleon-like ability to create across endlessly changing genres. From the mystical Far East to the very personification of one's paradise, chic elegance or pure whimsy, an Ed Libby experience appeals to all five senses.

For this chic soirée, the luxurious color of love served as a template for my design inspiration. Sultry scarlet crushed velvet dressed the guest tables and undulating banquette seating. I chose to mix dupioni silks and cherry red crocodile leather accents for dimensions of textures and tones. By suspending elaborate floral chandeliers, a feeling of intimacy may be created, even in a cavernous venue. Tall floral candelabras dripping in luxurious crimson blooms mixed with rich ruby vessels and warm flickering candlelight created an environment of pure elegance. Using a combination of edgy Plexiglass elements juxtaposed with lavish traditional touches brought out this couple's "Uptown elegance meets Soho chic" personality.

Photograph by Hechler Photographers

Photograph by Hechler Photographers

Photograph by Hechler Photographers

Above: A Lucite-covered swimming pool is awash with light from beneath and topped with an intricate botanical sculpture composed of highly stylized tiers of sumptuous orchids, green apples, eggplants, and lavish florals. A trickling water feature at the center lends tranquility to the atmosphere. I designed sculpted "flowerpot" cocktail tables with topiaries to add to the pure whimsy my client requested. Enchanted custom-built furniture vignettes provided fanciful repose for guests to imbibe in the beauty around them.

Facing page: I decided that the walls and ceiling of the tent would be draped in flowing fabrics; the floors were covered in plush coral carpeting, adding to the beauty of the environment. Each of the guest tables sat beneath a fabulous floral and crystal chandelier encrusted with lavish blooms, including roses and orchids in shades of amber, mango, and peach. Three floral spheres hung from the center of the chandelier while delicate candles and shimmering strung crystal strands streamed toward the table. Centered below the chandelier was a fragrant pool of water accented with floating candles and embraced in a floral collar. I selected a sumptuous coral-colored dupioni silk cloth with a shimmering sheer palette overlay trimmed in leopard eyelash to dress the table.

Photograph by Gruber Photographers

Photograph by Gruber Photographers

"I always tell my clients how important it is to incorporate at least one fabulous 'editorial moment' into every event; art for art's sake."

—Ed Libby

Left: For a very contemporary setting, we chose to wash the venue in color and sheer fabrics. The tables were dressed in white glossy patent leather cloths and topped with modern crystal vessels of varying heights, accented with romantic flickering candlelight. Sleek white liquid vinyl cylinders were artfully arranged and filled with clusters of hot pink calla lilies, roses, and hydrangeas with occasional touches of tangerine providing an extra pop of color.

Facing page: I am fortunate to have clients that appreciate elegance and are thrilled by originality. From an over-the-top gala to a Hollywood-themed event, I love the freedom of expression my clients allow. Customized set pieces, whether entry portals or lighting fixtures, create original moments at every signature event. Personalized center displays, tailored seating vignettes, and unique fabrics and color combinations mix for a truly unforgettable experience.

Previous pages: For a complete indoor winter white-out I began my design with volumes of billowing fabrics and wall-to-wall white carpeting to block all color from the venue. Transparent tables were lit from beneath, covered in sheer fabric and surrounded with Lucite Ghost Chairs. Soaring branches formed winter white trees that umbrellaed the guest tables, which were accented at their base with geometrical, stylized, white floral spheres glistening with mirrors and crystals. Votives cascaded from the branches and dotted the tabletop with flickering candlelight. The perimeter of the room was filled with natural branches and snow-flocked pine trees, which instantly transported guests to an opulent winter clearing in the middle of Manhattan.

Photograph by Fred Marcus Photography

Photograph by Fred Marcus Photography

Photograph by Fred Marcus Photography

Photograph by Hechler Photographers

Photograph by André Maier Photography

"I'm inspired by the idea that it's not what you do...it's what else you do."
—Ed Libby

Right: For a Hamptons-meets-Manhattan rehearsal dinner, I designed an intimate event in elegant whites with contrasting natural tones including fruitwood chairs, beeswax candles, and rattan chargers. The tables were dressed in crisp natural white linens with hemstitched napkins. Multilevel tablescapes were created using multitudes of candles and teak bento boxes filled with orchids, gardenias, roses, and lizianthus. Delicate stemware and place settings were topped with custom menus and placecards to complete this graceful yet stylized design.

Facing page: Although simplistic and sleek, this Asian-inspired atmosphere is composed of a myriad of intricate details. A soaring bamboo tower features orchids and foliage rising from a tranquil stone and candlelit base, serving as a focal point of the room. Sleek furniture, restrained florals, and illuminated majestic stands of bamboo complete the scene. Simple ingredients plus a flair for the dramatic equals Zen squared.

Photograph by Gruber Photographers

views

Each day, I have the opportunity to express myself through a unique art form for which I have an ever-growing passion. In order to create remarkable environments for my clients, I draw on life experiences: the journey of engaging all five senses, exploring new ideas, and collaborating with friends. I feel truly blessed to be able to share my gift with the world and take others on this fantastic voyage of exploration.

Square Root
ALEX AMIDI | JEFF JOHNSON

It sounds like the makings of a sitcom: rebellious surfer and Persian artist move to Orange County and open an event design company, where they work with a rotating cast of fascinating personalities to construct spectacular events. In reality, Jeff Johnson and Alex Amidi seemed drawn together by fate, each starting out in the floral design business and taking separate paths before meeting and founding their own business more than 10 years ago.

The pair started out in Jeff's garage; now they and Square Root's 30 full-time employees work out of a 20,000-square-foot studio in Irvine. Even though they average 200 events a year, they maintain a truly personal approach. Alex still constructs many of the flower arrangements himself, and Jeff insists on being involved with his hosts from start to finish. But this meticulous attention is only one part of Jeff and Alex's success; the other lies in their incredible talent for designing high-end boutique work on a large scale.

Self-described trendsetters, Alex and Jeff always strive to push their limits and not simply recycle previous ideas. Whether working from a theme, going with a single inspirational color, or designing based on only the vaguest notion, the results are unfailingly magnificent. Even the belt-tightening seen across the country from the recession hasn't impacted Square Root significantly. If anything, Jeff and Alex see the economic dip as a golden chance to up the creative ante. After all, opportunities often present themselves without warning, something the men of Square Root know how to appreciate.

To invoke a feeling of warmth and richness, we created a table that melded autumn colors with an Italian and Mediterranean aesthetic. The tree itself became a luscious bouquet of fruits and flowers, with pomegranates, grapes, dahlias, peonies, lilacs, and chocolate cosmos bursting forth from between the candles.

Photograph by Bleu Cotton Photography

Photograph by Victor Sizemore Photography

Photograph by Victor Sizemore Photography

"Good design should accomplish two things: be appreciated by everyone and stand the test of time."
—Jeff Johnson

Right and facing page bottom: Innovative lighting, custom-dyed suede chair covers, and creative table modifications brought the ocean indoors. The 100 tables were fitted with Lucite tops bearing square cut-outs; inside floated blue coral, candles, and vases brimming with orchids. State-of-the-art, wireless LED lights embedded in each cut-out fluctuated between aqua blue and teal green, giving the impression of dining underwater. Unable to remove the room's chandeliers, we disguised their contrasting style by removing the shades and overlaying geometric fabric frames, which gave the impression of twinkling stars.

Facing page top: It's practically a rule that when you have a stunning view of the ocean, you do everything you can not to block it out. A 12-by-12 acrylic altar gave us something from which to suspend flowers, but kept the sightlines open for the guests. Flower mounds and oversized silver garden gazing balls lined the aisle, imparting a chic, linear, and unexpected effect. As a considerate touch, matching blankets were provided for each guest on a rather chilly day.

Photograph by Victor Sizemore Photography

Photograph by John Solano Photography

Photograph by Bleu Cotton Photography

Above: A contemporary Indian wedding, Malibu's Saddleback Ranch, Cirque du Soleil, and a head table 36 feet long. With ingredients like this, how could the event not be fabulous? Even though the tent was constructed on a grassy lawn, we built raised platforms to ensure everyone had a clear view of the performers. The couple wanted a slick, Miami nightclub vibe, but we tweaked certain aspects—like the length of the head table—to incorporate the large amount of family present. Wanting to make a statement with the chandelier, it was 20 feet in diameter and strung with white globes and hot pink and white orchid leis.

Facing page left: Featured on the TV show "Platinum Weddings," the Art Deco-inspired event worked in harmony with the architectural and design elements already in place at L.A.'s Millennium Biltmore Hotel. After altering the color scheme slightly to match the elaborate ballroom carpets, we projected scarlet and peacock blue spotlights on the columns, carrying the theme all the way up to the ceiling. Hand-painted silver vases encased in rhinestones and black satin ribbons each held 250 stems of hand-opened roses.

Facing page top: The view from the sweetheart table encompassed a mini-wall of roses, black Art Deco mirrors reflecting the band, and four panels of tufted leather to give the stage a classic, Old Hollywood feel.

Facing page bottom: The huppah was covered in hand-pleated cerulean chiffon and lit from within with ruby red lights. An archway of candles framed the huppah's centerpiece: a cloth inscribed with congratulations and well wishes from the couple's friends and family.

Previous pages: While the rose-covered mandap, or Hindu wedding canopy, commanded attention at 12 feet wide and 14 feet tall, a multitude of intricate details sprinkled throughout the room provided surprise and delight for the guests. Hand-pleated silk chair covers resembling the back of the bride's dress, custom candelabras from India, jeweled butterfly napkin rings from New York—everything was custom and all of it was opulent.

Photograph by Karen French Photography

Photograph by Karen French Photography

Photograph by Karen French Photography

Photograph by Joe Photo

"Even if your event is not extravagant, have one thing that makes a definite statement."

—Alex Amidi

Right: A simple entry table outside the reception room runs the risk of appearing static, so by securing 300 roses to the vase and having orchids, hydrangeas, and tulips spilling out from the top, the table seems almost like a living creature. Standing at nearly 10 feet tall, the table was a taste of what awaited guests inside.

Facing page: Juxtaposing romantic roses with modern fixtures and a striking color palette gives a design added visual interest.

Photograph by Joe Latter Photography

views

Picking a designer for your event should be like picking a contractor for your home. Experience is obviously important, but it's crucial not to base your decision on who's the cheapest or who has the prettiest delivery vans. Do they employ enough staff to execute your event in a timely manner? Do they know the vendors well enough to work smoothly with them? Do you get the feeling they might highjack your dream and make it all about them? Use referrals and resources to make sure you're comfortable.

IMAGES BY LIGHTING

RAYMOND THOMPSON | CURT STAHL

In the early 1980s, Images by Lighting was practically the only game in town. Founded by Raymond Thompson, a former electrical engineer whose hobby was lighting, the event lighting production and design company is now a Los Angeles powerhouse. Providing dramatic lightscapes for entertainment award show parties, celebrity bashes, cultural galas, and corporate and charity events, Images by Lighting's signature touch can be experienced at hundreds of high-profile gatherings throughout Southern California.

To build Images into the well-respected and admired company it is today, Raymond has relied on a mixture of creativity, efficiency, friendliness, and professionalism. Joining him in these pursuits is Curt Stahl, who came on board in 1992 and now serves as partner. Together, Raymond and Curt find the fun in their work, channeling their passion to transform spaces through carefully constructed power distribution, lighting design, and video and still image projection.

When hosts first come to Images by Lighting, they may not have a fully realized understanding about their lighting needs. But the trust that Raymond and Curt inspire continually results in thrilled hosts and astonished guests, fueling the Images team to consistently raise the bar. In the years that have passed since its inaugural season, Images by Lighting has served as something of a mentor to several young lighting designers, many who have then gone on to form their own companies. As the first and ultimate example of passion and professionalism in the lighting business, Images by Lighting has ensured those apprentices learned from the best.

We relied on a palette of lavender, amethyst, and deep plum to create mystery for an Indonesian-themed Emmy party. Something we're known for is disguising the equipment so it blends seamlessly into the decor, even if that means painting the lighting fixtures to match their surroundings. A lot of people wouldn't put forth that kind of effort, but for us it's not even a question.

Photograph © Gabor Ekecs

Photograph by Michael Haight

Photograph © Gabor Ekecs

Photograph by Brian Callaway

Photograph by Nadine Froger, courtesy of Sequoia Productions

Above: The 60th Primetime Emmy Awards® Governors Ball was the diamond celebration for the famed party, so we worked with the Academy's art directors to come up with a fitting design. The chandeliers emulated stacks of diamonds, and a black background was lit with LED lights that replicated the astrological constellations.

Facing page top left: Light doesn't have to be a static element; in fact, we love to work with shifting light, which creates constant visual interest and provides an element of surprise for the guests. Working off of a "Wizard of Oz" theme, the ceiling became a sinuous rainbow, where the light was shot through peacock feathers to create an intricate pattern.

Facing page top right: A collection of South American art was the main focus at an HBO party. We created an attractive background that kept the flavor of the evening yet didn't detract from the sculptures.

Facing page bottom: A cocktail party held in a former cathedral provided a pristine white background and lots of architectural details—basically a lighting designer's dream.

"Lighting produces emotion. There's a direct relationship between light, color, and the human condition."
—Curt Stahl

Photograph courtesy of FIDM

Above and left: We do a lot of collaborative work with the Fashion Institute of Design & Merchandising in L.A., and its runway shows are always a treat. By working hand-in-hand with the school's art department and in-house video support team, we are given the opportunity to create interactive, attention-grabbing environments to showcase the students' hard work.

Facing page top: Besides enveloping the locally resourced drapes and chandeliers with indigo light at a beach event in Quixmala, Mexico, we illuminated the crashing ocean surf with aquamarine to enhance its nighttime beauty.

Facing page bottom: HBO's Golden Globes party was held directly behind the ballroom where the award show had just finished, so we joined the two events by projecting video imagery on the shared wall. A video DJ manipulated the animation in time with the music, while rotating daisy gobos danced on the floor.

Photograph courtesy of FIDM

Photograph courtesy of Special Occasions

Photograph © Gabor Ekecs

Photograph by Nadine Froger, courtesy of Sequoia Productions

"Always have a backup plan. Maximize your success by including a redundant generator and standby technician."

—Raymond Thompson

Right: A chandelier created by the event designer that measured 12 feet across was lit entirely by LED lights and gelled fluorescents. The LEDs were programmed to sequence color throughout the evening. The discs were actually made from fisheye mirrors, so not only could guests see their own reflections above the bar, they could see the entire room.

Facing page: Everything about the 61st Primetime Emmy Awards® Governors Ball was big, bright, and colorful: The beaded crystal columns were 30 feet tall, the chandelier 14 feet across, and the lanterns 8 feet high. The beginning of the party was actually very monochromatic, but as the event progressed, the colors would "chase each other" through the room, resulting in a candy-colored dream by the night's end.

Photograph by Nadine Froger Photography

views

Don't hold back when describing your vision to your lighting designer. And, if possible, always try to get your lighting supplier and designer involved in the initial planning stages. This will always result in a more cohesive design. With the amount of technology available today and a little imagination, the possibilities are endless!

KAREN TRAN FLORALS
KAREN TRAN

Every event host is unique. Each has his or her own particular tastes, style, and specific needs. Some may tend toward a modern and contemporary theme while others might prefer classic, traditional décor. Some are drawn to the beach, others to formal ballrooms. By understanding the host's vision for the event, Karen Tran makes the floral arrangements flow with and accentuate an occasion's central theme.

As a child, Karen was surrounded by gardens and the beauty of nature. Her love for flowers stemmed from this early upbringing, and later her talent for floral arranging began to emerge. Karen worked with blooms and stems part-time until the mid-1990s, when she took the leap and went full time with her own company. Now her sumptuous floral creations grace events in the Southern California area and also around the world.

Karen is a master at tuning in to a host's likes and dislikes. She then executes a well-thought out design that works in harmony with the event's venue, budget, season, and theme. By taking the viewpoint of both the host and their guests, she maximizes the impact of her designs, while still retaining intimate personal meaning. A grandmother's antique jewelry set, for example, can be worked into a bride's bouquet. Whether dazzling, elaborate, or simply lovely, Karen's flower sculptures bear a unique hallmark of elegance.

Extravagance is my signature. I like creating lush, lavish designs. For one wedding ceremony design, I used almost 3,000 roses to craft a flower petal aisle lined with rose pomanders.

Photograph by Darin Fong Photography

Photograph by Karen Tran

Photograph by Darin Fong Photography

Photograph by Terri Rippee Photography

Above and right: I used gold, lace, silk, and a profusion of cascading roses and blooming peonies to compose the Versailles theme—a design ornate enough for a queen.

Facing page: For my own wedding held on the grounds of the Hotel del Coronado, my husband built an exquisite canopy to shelter our exchange of vows. He incorporated an antique chandelier; it now hangs in our home as a reminder of that special moment. Romantic canopies, personalized hand-painted runners, and other ceremonial keepsakes are becoming increasingly popular as after-wedding mementos.

Photograph by Terri Rippee Photography

Photograph by Studio 7 Photography

Photograph by Darin Fong Photography

Incorporating crystal is an excellent way to add radiance to the table. As lights dim and candles grow brighter, the jewels among the blooms are enchanting.

Photograph by Darin Fong Photography

"Each design should be lovely, vibrant, and full of details, but most importantly, it should tell a story and captivate the viewer."

—Karen Tran

Photograph by Darin Fong Photography

Photograph by Darin Fong Photography

Photograph by Darin Fong Photography

Photograph by Darin Fong Photography

Photograph by Darin Fong Photography

Photograph by Darin Fong Photography

"Trends come and go, but some hosts will always be drawn to a more traditional and classic design motif."

—Karen Tran

A fresh approach to traditional bouquets: Innovations like a nautilus shell brimming with orchids or a flower girl basket constructed entirely of rosebuds and rhinestones make memorable impressions.

Photograph by Darin Fong Photography

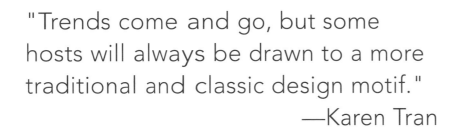

views

When crafting extravagant floral arrangements for an occasion, it's vital to gather as much input as possible from the host. Through focused consultation, the whole story and central theme can be expressed through all the various design details. I have a true passion for my art form. I paint through the colors of the flowers and sculpt through the shape of the blossoms to create exquisite events.

Nisie's Enchanted Florist, Inc.

NISIE VORACHARD

An enchanting event begins with a delightful, magical ambience. Yet it is more than that. It is a celebration that speaks to the hearts of everyone involved, clearly expressing the host's personality and effervescing with the very essence of the host's fantasy. For Nisie, this enchantment is won or lost in the floral design.

Nisie's respect for the blooms' beauty stems from her childhood in Thailand, where her family owned an orchard farm and grew flowers in its unused land. This connection with nature and the beautiful process of growth continued to reside with Nisie through her move to the United States and her immensely successful career in fashion. Through a simple act of kindness in designing the floral décor for a friend's wedding, Nisie was encouraged to transition into a new industry. In 1996, Nisie's Enchanted Florist was born and has since expanded to include a boutique retail studio.

With an undying desire to try something new for every project, Nisie has developed her floral design into a renowned art. A two-hour initial consultation, which includes browsing through potential props and accessories for design ideas, helps Nisie better understand the event host and his or her personality, style, and goals, drawing out the nuances that will set the event apart from countless others. From being a featured florist in *Grace Ormonde* to celebrity weddings, corporate celebrations, and private ceremonies, Nisie unites texture and color to forge elegant creations that gently push the envelope.

Inspired by the linens, which carried a very Dior feel with a hint of vintage style, and the private château setting, I created a feminine, romantic look. Mercury glass with gold detailing establishes a timeless quality. A mix of sizes, heights, textures, and elements adds interest for every angle and glance.

Photograph by Eckman Maus Photography

Photograph by Barnaby Draper Studios

Photograph by Eckman Maus Photography

Photograph by Mike Colón Photographers

Photograph by TripleCord Photography

Regardless of the event's ambience, I always include an unexpected element in the design. Whether it's an eye-catching cake suspended from the ceiling framed by 12-foot-tall trees or the vertical elements of nature juxtaposed against horizontally placed manzanita branches atop Lucite stands—or even the addition of pearls or hanging globes to an arrangement—something must elicit an unanticipated feeling for the design to really pop.

" Allowing yourself to become comfortable in design is really the end of creativity. "

—Nisie Vorachard

Photograph by Anderson Photography

"A monochromatic scheme makes a bold statement whether using many elements or just a few."

—Nisie Vorachard

Above: At the Pacific Design Center, the clean lines of the exterior and contemporary landscaping prompted me to design an ultramodern setting that challenged my usual look. A Lucite table showed off the brilliant colors of orchids, miniature calla lilies, hydrangeas, and wheatgrass.

Facing page: For a bride who loved red, a tone-on-tone theme perfectly merged with accents depicting her Asian heritage. The intricate floral aisle runner, lined with grab boxes, bamboo, and cherry blossoms, led to a romantically draped rotunda with fabric, lanterns, and orchid garlands. The reception's monochromatic hue made a huge statement of warmth and romance.

Photograph by Chris Humphrey Photography

Photograph by Chris Humphrey Photography

Photograph by Chris Humphrey Photography

Photograph by Aaron Delesie Photography

Photograph by Aaron Delesie Photography

Photograph by Aaron Delesie Photography

"A good designer can work with any request while still inserting a piece of his or her own signature look."

—Nisie Vorachard

A soft, romantic look, for example, can be interpreted in many ways. In one event, romantic translated into a lush, Tuscan, *A Midsummer Night's Dream* feel, complete with hedges lining the aisle, lots of texture, varying layers for the centerpieces, and a combination of different flowers. In contrast, a more contemporary ceremony exhibited romance in clean lines and asymmetrical placements of the nearly 60 containers holding roses.

Photograph by Aaron Delesie Photography

views

Don't compromise on the flowers and décor at the reception or in the main space of the event. This is where guests will spend most of their time and where the hosts will be able to enjoy the setting. Take the opportunity to truly express yourself and make a statement.

BARTKRESA DESIGN
BART KRESA

Growing up in Poland, it seemed as though Bart Kresa's life would be firmly committed to music. But while later working as a professional musician, he unearthed a camera in his father's garage and immediately fell in love. He went on to attend art school for photography in the early 1990s, and was fascinated when he discovered large-scale projection. Now Bart has become the undisputed master of projection design, even teaching the first-ever class offered for architectural projection at the University of Arts in Philadelphia. BARTKRESA design, a collaboration between Bart Kresa and Peter Schroff, has a simple approach: absorb the project, grasp the desired results, explore the possibilities, and produce something that communicates, touches, and inspires.

All of the work is architecturally specific, carefully constructed to highlight certain structural elements while displaying a pictorial motif on other areas. What is magnificent on one building would look entirely out of place on another. Bart works closely with an event's lighting designers to determine the correct number of projectors needed, as well as where to place them. This careful collaboration is mutually beneficial; the lighting designers know how best to proceed during an event, and Bart can ensure accurate color, saturation, and contrast.

For Bart, each new venture is a chance to create fresh, original temporary art, and his work has been marveled at worldwide. In 2009, he designed a projection environment that won a major award by the International Association of Amusement Parks and Attractions. Bart works hard to keep his business sustainable by reusing equipment and creating as little waste as possible.

To honor 35 years of diplomatic relationship between Austria and China, 150 Chinese and 250 Austrian artists took part in a TV show called "Salzburg bei Nacht," or "Salzburg at Night," that aired on Chinese television and was viewed by 400 million people. My projection highlighted one of the city's most recognizable landmarks, the Salzburg Cathedral.

Photograph by Bart Kresa

Photograph by Bart Kresa

Photograph by Bart Kresa

Photograph by Bart Kresa

Photograph by Manuel Reta III

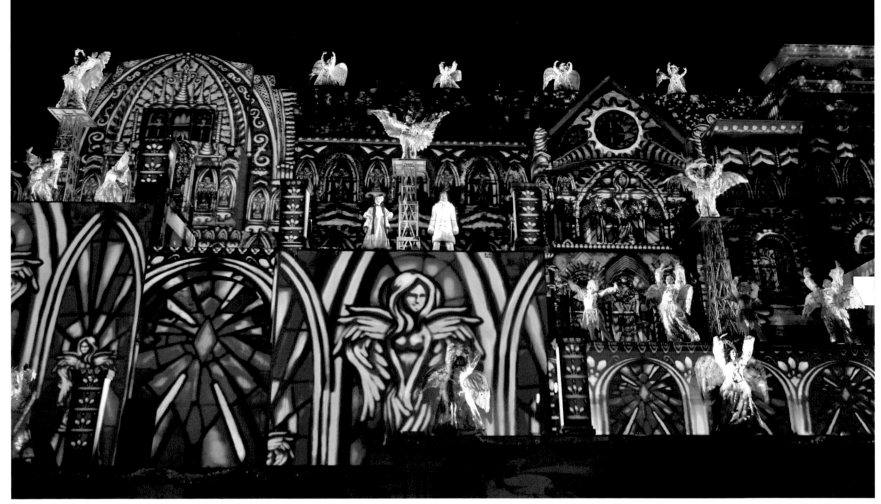

Photograph by Bart Kresa

Photograph by Bart Kresa

Photograph by Bart Kresa

Photograph by Bart Kresa

"Projection design is a fleeting illusion, art that doesn't really exist."
—Bart Kresa

Right: As part of the inauguration of the Polish Year and to salute the people of Israel for their 60th anniversary of the State of Israel, the facade of the Municipal Building in Tel Aviv was turned into an amazing light spectacle for one night.

Facing page top: A kaleidoscopic display of L.A.'s diverse landmarks rotated, disappeared, and resurfaced throughout the night in a display of high-intensity video projection inside the tent for the L.A. Area Chamber of Commerce 120th Inaugural Dinner.

Facing page bottom: For the opening of the Home Depot Center Soccer Arena, home of the L.A. Galaxy, the wraparound projection was created in a 120-by-200-foot tent outside the arena. All of the projection gear was set up outside of the tent, with projections directed through openings in the walls. This created an ambience without obstructing the space with equipment.

Previous pages: It's truly amazing the transformations that occur as soon as the lights are switched on. Suddenly there's art where before there was only blank space. Instead of relying on traditional set pieces, a Christmas show in Osaka, Japan, used my projections to create 12 different environments, each featuring a very distinctive look and color.

Photograph by Bart Kresa

views

For many years we have been at the forefront of projection design, partly because of the many tools I've designed that help us do the work more efficiently and with greater clarity. Every project we do is unique, and I love coming up with new ideas all the time.

The Hidden Garden

Amy Child Marella

For Amy Child Marella, her work—and her idea of fun—doesn't truly begin until she's visited the Los Angeles Flower Market. With nearly two blocks packed with gorgeous flowers in every color imaginable, the market pulls Amy in to browse Mother Nature's latest offerings, searching and selecting the perfect blooms for each of her projects.

This visual and fragrant journey provides Amy and her team at The Hidden Garden with inspiration to craft everything from the perfect boutonnière to jaw-dropping centerpieces. Rooted in a collaborative effort with the event host and all of the professionals, the process of design takes shape amidst a bustling but Zen-like atmosphere where the word "no" is rarely spoken. With nary a job too small to take on or problem too big to surmount, the unstated maxim centers on the host's ultimate satisfaction, regardless of the cost or effort.

Behind this philosophy is Amy's addiction to perfection. To achieve flawless outcomes, The Hidden Garden applies a system that is extremely organized—to the point that every event could run smoothly without Amy because of her detailed notes and planning—and staff members who possess specific areas of expertise to cover the entire design spectrum. In the end, what makes the difference between a so-so floral design and one crafted by Amy or one of her designers is their personal relationship with the event host, which naturally prompts a passion for and dedication to the project.

A neutral, unembellished space at the Pacific Design Center led us to take a modern, elegant approach. We injected a pop of color with the fuchsia orchids and brought in a contemporary flair with symmetrical arrangements in sleek glass vases.

Photograph by Vernon T. Williams

Photograph by David Michael Photography

Photograph by David Michael Photography

I had been excitedly waiting to use elephants made of brightly colored thread at just the right event. So when we started on the Indian tablescape at the Four Seasons Hotel at Westlake Village, I knew these elements would be the ideal inspiration. In collaboration with Raj Tents and Wildflower Linen, we established a fabulous setting with an abundance of color and texture. The warm, animated colors of roses, marigolds, cymbidium and mokara orchids, hydrangeas, and dahlia, interspersed with a few green Fuji mums created a pavé look but with a bit more punctuation. The shimmer from the gold containers made everything sparkle, and the turquoise candle accents expanded the color palette.

Photograph by David Michael Photography

Photograph by Cheri Pearl Photography

Photograph by Cheri Pearl Photography

Photograph by Cheri Pearl Photography

Photograph by Cheri Pearl Photography

Photograph by Cheri Pearl Photography

"Monochromatic arrangements are all about texture and abundance."
—Amy Child Marella

Floral creations don't always have to be flowery. For a trendy, modern host who preferred a clean look for her spring reception, Lisa Vorce with Oh, How Charming! coordinated a green and brown color palette. We arranged wheatgrass, dogwood blooms, viburnum, cymbidium orchids, monkey tail, and limes for the centerpieces and brought the color toward the guest with a kermit mum on each napkin.

views

Work with someone you feel comfortable collaborating with, who you can engage in back and forth communication to draw out your goals and desires. Along with having an open mind, good communication with all of your event professionals is the most important element to create a perfect celebration.

kool. Party Rentals

JACK WEINER

White furniture can be a nightmare to keep clean, but imagine a huge warehouse where half the inventory is comprised of snow white furniture and crystal-clear acrylic pieces. Instead of keeping them under a glass dome, untouched by appetizer crumbs and droplets of wine, kool. Party Rentals transports this pristine décor to parties around the country where it always arrives—believe it or not—pristine. How does this company manage to keep an entire collection of white furniture white when one piece is usually enough to do most people in? The miracle-working team at kool. Party Rentals, led by owner Jack Weiner, maintains every bit of its contemporary, modern event furniture and illuminated décor in-house, utilizing custom-built protective carts and some extreme deep cleaning.

Officially formed in 2006, kool. Party Rentals evolved out of Jack's experiences as a corporate event producer. After bringing in trucks full of furniture from three different cities for a single party, Jack realized there was a niche just waiting to be filled. Starting with only eight illuminated cocktail tables, kool. has since grown into a boutique company that has provided versatile, eco-friendly event furniture for events as wide-ranging as Super Bowl VIP post-game parties and NBA All-Star Game events to private celebrity functions and festivities at the Playboy Mansion. But it's not just its wizardry with white fabric that has distinguished kool.; a fun, laid-back company atmosphere paired with tight attention to detail has cemented its reputation as a favorite among hosts.

All of our products use wireless, battery-operated, remote-controlled LED lights, which means longer usage times, less heat emitted, and no wires to trip over. Because the batteries are rechargeable, we consume hardly any energy, but we purchase carbon offsets for what we do consume. This is definitely the direction the event industry is going, and based on the limitless creative ways to use products such as our viewboxes and acrylic candelabras, it's not only ecologically smart but beautiful.

Photograph by Resolusean Photography

Photograph by Happy Photos

Photograph by Happy Photos

Photograph by Happy Photos

Photograph by Goldstein Photography

Many of our products are interchangeable, stackable, and modular. White acrylic bases can be arranged into countless formations and the same items can appear completely different based on how they've been assembled. A splitback furniture piece can transform into a daybed as easily as it becomes a fully upright sofa, showing its versatility and multi-functionality.

Photograph by kool. Party Rentals

Photograph by kool. Party Rentals

Photograph by kool. Party Rentals

"Transforming a space requires a vision, and bringing that vision to life requires the perfect blend of furniture, décor, fabrics, and creative lighting design."

—Jack Weiner

Furniture can really determine the tone of the room, but it can also help shake things up and present something unexpected to the guests. Positioning pieces traditionally meant for lounging, like sofas and daybeds, in a theater formation to hear a speech or watch a presentation instantly adds a sense of playfulness. Placing crisp stuffed chairs outdoors amongst spiky greenery or on a lush, grassy lawn is unexpected but appreciated.

Photograph by Kelvin Photography

views

We get more calls and compliments about our delivery people than I ever thought possible. While most hosts think they're just ordering furniture and décor, really so much depends on the dedicated people who do the transporting, set up, and dismantling.

LIGHTEN UP, INC.

NATHAN MEGAW

The linens may be custom, the crystal may be flawless, and the flowers may be perfect, but seeing a room flooded with flickering, unflattering fluorescent light means only one thing: the mood has officially been killed. Lighting plays an essential part in any special event, so much so that an entire carefully crafted atmosphere can disappear with a simple flick of a switch. One company understands the importance of lighting better than most, mainly because it's owned and operated by skilled and experienced technicians. Lighten Up was formed in 2002 by Nathan Megaw, a man who patiently paid his dues by working his way from technician to designer to president of his own company.

Placing a high priority on excellent communication and an impeccable work ethic has caused elated hosts to return time and again. Lighten Up has designed for a wide range of events, including numerous Golden Globe and Oscar parties. But even if a celebration is a little more intimate and doesn't include your 1,500 closest friends, the technicians and designers are experts at working with any budget and level of host involvement. As they've found, even the simplest color wash or the addition of pin spots can completely transform a room. More complex designs can become part of the décor, as integral to the ambience as furniture or music. Whatever the event, Lighten Up can help make sure the mood matches the occasion.

A silent auction and fundraiser for the Autry National Center allowed us to play up Gene Autry's beloved image as "The Singing Cowboy." Stars were scattered across the walls and ceiling while pin spots illuminated the tables.

Photograph by Line 8 Photography

Photograph by Line 8 Photography

Photograph courtesy of Lighten Up, Inc.

Lighting is extremely versatile; something as simple at uplighting columns in an unexpected shade or projecting an unusual pattern on the walls or ceiling can entirely change a room's dynamic. Stackable cubes lit from within by LEDs produce a uniform glow from all angles.

Photograph by Line 8 Photography

Photograph courtesy of Lighten Up, Inc.

Photograph courtesy of Lighten Up, Inc.

Photograph courtesy of Lighten Up, Inc.

"It's essential to understand the value and ambience that lighting can create."

—Nathan Megaw

As a way to enhance or draw attention to special moments, lighting is extremely effective. A subtle shift in brightness or color, or the addition of playful gobo projections, can communicate to your guests that something important is about to happen.

Photograph courtesy of Lighten Up, Inc

views

How a company handles proposals and administrative work is a tremendous indicator of how reliable they will be further on down the road. Waiting to receive answers might be a sign that they don't understand your needs, or that they may show up late or with missing equipment on your big day. To avoid this, always have your initial meeting in person; it's worth taking the time and energy to meet the vendor face to face. You can tell a lot about a company's professionalism from those first 15 minutes.

PETERSON EVENT LIGHTING

BRANDON PETERSON

It seems like most everyone in Los Angeles used to be an actor, and Brandon Peterson is no exception. Nowadays, however, the owner of Peterson Event Lighting can be found programming spotlights instead of basking in them. After segueing into the lighting business by chance more than 10 years ago, Brandon discovered he possessed a natural talent for the work and formed his own company in 2004. Many weddings, corporate events, and Hollywood wrap parties later, Peterson Event Lighting has established itself as the ideal company to illuminate life's most memorable moments.

Perhaps owing to his creative past, Brandon's approach to lighting design is more comparable to that of an artist's than an electrician's. "Painting an environment," as Brandon describes it, is his way of creating the mood for an event, be it formal, funky, or extravagant. In a city that parties every night, there's no shortage of competition for Peterson Event Lighting, but that's exactly what motivates the team to keep the inspiration flowing.

To make sure hosts aren't left in the dark when it comes to their lighting, the skilled staff at Peterson Event Lighting assumes total control, designing, constructing, and executing the unexpected—sometimes even for them. It's not uncommon for Brandon to arrive at an event and see some of the decorations, design elements, and colors for the first time. Rather than derail the process, this fresh perspective prompts inspiration and, in true artistic fashion, the results often exceed the initial design.

A rustic wedding that was designed around dark plaid linens and prickly antler chandeliers needed a soft glow for balance. A sprinkling of candlelight and strategically placed pin spots tempered the heaviness and drew attention to the romantic pops of color from the floral arrangements.

Photograph by Simone and Martin Photography

Photograph by Simone and Martin Photography

Photograph by Simone and Martin Photography

Photograph by Simone and Martin Photography

Photograph by Nadine Froger Photography

Photograph by Brandon Peterson

Above: After-parties are happening more and more, so it's a fun challenge to design lights for a formal, elegant room and then go the opposite direction and create a space with a hipper, trendier vibe. Sometimes the two areas are set up directly next to each other with only a curtain separating them, hinting at the late-night fun that is going to happen later.

Above right: One sure-fire way to transform a dance floor from a basic room element into a design statement is with lighting. Washing the floor with a cherry red glow, speckling it with white lights to resemble snowfall, and pairing it with hanging Tivoli columns gave the room thematic interest both above and below eye-level.

Facing page top and bottom right: Your guests don't just magically appear at the party, so take the opportunity to make an impact and continue the decorations on the outside, too. We projected a broken leaf pattern on the path leading to the reception area and uplit the 60 surrounding trees for a more striking welcome. Outdoor chandeliers added instant drama, and the reflection from the nearby lake multiplied the glittering results.

Facing page bottom left: To generate the shadowy feel of an ultra-exclusive club for a wedding after-party, decadent indigo lighting and shrouded chandeliers made the space much more intimate. Placing a tube of blue lights in front of the couches immediately designated the VIP area.

"When it comes to their lights, the host shouldn't have to be that involved. It's the designer's responsibility to make everything perfect for them."

—Brandon Peterson

Photograph by Jay Lawrence Goldman

Photograph by Simone and Martin Photography

Photograph by Brandon Peterson

Photograph by Simone and Martin Photography

"Since it's impossible to be everywhere at once, you really have to trust your team. After all, you can't change a light bulb in the middle of a party."

—Brandon Peterson

Right: I'll often come up with ideas and have them in my head for months or even years before I get the opportunity to use them. A bar mitzvah that centered around the film "Forrest Gump" provided many different theme rooms, but the entrance was an opportunity to make lighting part of the décor. With only yellow lanterns to work with, I stacked and connected them to different dimming channels to create a moving bubble effect. The fabric-draped tent supports were uplit with yellow and white bulbs—also on dimmers—so one side got brighter as the other darkened. The iconic smiley face image not only changed between yellow and white, it also rotated and moved up and down the stairs, ushering guests toward the reception tent.

Facing page: When you take into account the furniture, flowers, decorations, table settings, and linens—that's already a lot going on! My job is to accentuate all the different components without overpowering any of them, cohesively highlighting not only what was brought into the space for the event, but sometimes the architecture of the room as well.

Photograph by Curtis Dahl, Dahl Photography

views

For all of the planning and research that hosts put into their events, it's surprising how little importance most people place on their lights. Relying on before-and-after pictures of past events is the most effective way I've found to communicate the incredible transformative powers of lighting. After all, nothing ruins a mood quicker than overhead fluorescent lights running at full blast.

PLATINUM PRO
TRENT SMILEY

While a sign of a good party may be a packed dance floor, a customized dance floor is an inimitable canvas that will captivate your guests. The team at Platinum Pro took notice of the conventional, often bland dance floors being trucked in for parties and weddings and began inventing ways to produce stylish, customizable, yet budget-friendly dance floors. Thanks to an indispensable patent-pending rig and method designed by owner Trent Smiley, Platinum Pro discovered an effective formula for constructing the floors. Soon after he launched Platinum Pro in 2006, Trent branched out to include furniture rentals, event lighting, and much more to become one of Southern California's premier production companies.

The process is simple: Platinum Pro starts by establishing a budget based on the amount of people at the event and location. From there the design team creates a customized motif that might include images, monograms, inscriptions, logos, or borders that coordinate with the event's theme and décor. Set up of the floors depends on the complexity, but when finished the effect is seamless, without the joints and cracks normally seen on more traditional wood-paneled dance floors. The configuration of the floor can be round, square, oval, heart-shaped, or your own custom shape. Platinum Pro has even accommodated requests to turn floors into hockey rinks and football fields. No design is ever used twice, which not only ensures originality but also a pristine, gorgeous surface free of scuffs or dents. But once the guests get to boogying, all bets are off.

Besides owning the company, I also do most of the initial meetings and installations for that personal touch. I've found that hosts like the security of knowing they are dealing directly with the owner.

Photograph by Shawna Yarbourgh, Studio 7

Photograph by VCS Photography

Photograph by Tim Otto

Photograph by Lauren Ong

While white and gold tend to be wedding favorites, bold, unexpected colors make an impact. Few people realize it, but we can put literally anything on the dance floor. Magazine covers and logos, no matter how complex or detailed, look terrific at a larger scale and are ideal for corporate events.

"If you personalize cakes, florals, and linens, why not dance floors?"

—Trent Smiley

Photograph by Paul Barnett

Photograph by Bobby Earle

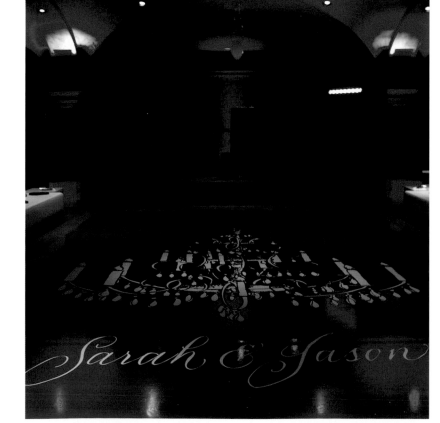

Photograph by Tim Otto

Photograph by Boyd Harris

Photograph by Boyd Harris

"What can be put on a customized dance floor? Anything the mind can imagine, but it's up to the DJ or band to get people dancing on it."

—Trent Smiley

The first year we averaged five floors, and each year it kept doubling. Now we do around 50 floors, by far exceeding any expectations I had when we started. Once it's patented, I'd like to market my rig and methods to other companies, giving people all over the country the option to use customizable dance floors. We may not be the ones building the floor for a party in New York, but our technology would be making it possible.

views

Package deals really do save you a lot of money, not to mention stress. Part of the reason I expanded Platinum Pro to include lighting and furniture rentals was so I could offer people a savings if they used me for more than one service. It also helps to remember that the fewer people there are in charge, the less chance there is of something going wrong.

RESOURCE ONE INC.

ROBERTA KARSCH

From the very beginning, Roberta Karsch knew she could never settle for being anything other than boutique and fabulous. A leader in couture linens, Roberta set herself and Resource One Inc. on a legendary journey by establishing only the highest standards. Initially, it was never in her game plan to be in the event rental business. But as she ventured into the world of corporate events, she discovered that hosts were more interested in renting her linens than buying them and she decided to take a chance.

Although she opened Resource One Inc. in 1990, Roberta's experience with luxury goods and textiles goes back several more years. She worked a decade in product development for Nordstrom, traveling the world and seeking out interior design items, antiques, and an eclectic mix of gifts to serve as inspiration for the department store's private label. After graduating from what she cheekily calls the "University of Nordstrom," Roberta transitioned into textile design, creating primarily for the interior design industry. With her flawless taste level and access to excellent materials, it quickly became apparent that Roberta possessed the tools to create something remarkable. Since opening, Resource One Inc. has provided the linens for countless entertainment and high profile events, most notably the Academy Awards® Governors Ball since the early 1990s. By remaining small and select, Resource One Inc. has maintained its exquisite craftsmanship and meticulous attention to detail, the very definition of boutique fabulous.

Each year, the planning for the upcoming Governors Ball begins with a concept, and the selection of textiles early on is critical to the overall design. The 82nd Annual Academy Awards® Governors Ball, with production and design by Sequoia Productions, featured our luminescent Champagne Glitter Dot Tulle design. Part of what gives these cloths the "wow" factor is that each circle detail at the hemline is cut by hand.

Photograph by Norma Lopez Molina

Photograph by Raul Vega

Although we can design to satisfy any whim, my own personal style is very tailored and contemporary. The crisp edges paired with luxurious fabrics such as velvet, silk, and taffeta create a gorgeous contrast and an added level of visual interest. We can also provide chairs, lighting, and decorative accessories, which helps to cement a whole look.

Photograph by Norma Lopez Molina

Photograph by Line 8 Photography

Photograph by Nadine Froger Photography

"If you're going to be special, you really need to be special. Your designs need to be so fabulous that they can sell themselves."

—Roberta Karsch

With the ever-changing Oscars themes we get the opportunity to try to top ourselves every year. The introduction of Bourgie lamps for the 80th Annual Academy Awards® Governors Ball, with production and design by Sequoia Productions, and custom-trimmed raw silk runners for the 81st Annual Academy Awards® Governors Ball, also with production and design by Sequoia Productions, let us play with different textures, color palettes, and materials.

Photograph by Mike Colón

views

Some people say that style is subjective; it can be temporary, a passing fashion. But real style will always encompass classic design and color, and we love to fuse the two. We've learned that putting different elements together to achieve the unexpected is what attracts people to us, but what continually brings them back is our quality of construction. For example, we never use a merrow finish on an item—everything is perfectly hemmed, trimmed, and merchandised cohesively. That attention to detail and pride in our work represents who we are.

Eric Buterbaugh Designs

ERIC BUTERBAUGH

If you're in Eric Buterbaugh's studio at the Four Seasons Hotel in Beverly Hills and Demi Moore walks in for a chat, don't be surprised. Eric often says he creates his opulent floral arrangements mainly for friends; what he doesn't add is that his circle of friends includes such marquee names as Tobey Maguire, Salma Hayek, Gwen Stefani, and the ageless Ms. Moore and her husband Ashton Kutcher.

Eric got his start in the business thanks to a friend who asked him to put together a few centerpieces for a party she was throwing. When she was later flooded with calls inquiring who had done the stunning designs, Eric took it as a sign. After having worked in fashion in London and Italy for years, most notably with Gianni Versace, Eric returned to the states and opened his studio at the plush Four Seasons around 2000. As he points out, he works with exciting hosts, so the opportunity to develop innovative new trends and put together imaginative designs is enormous. In his frequent travels, Eric has even noticed techniques he developed years ago popping up all over the world.

A signature of Eric's is his uncanny ability to immediately identify a person's unique style. Whether that person is a celebrity or not, incredible attention to detail and perfect assembly are evident in everything Eric delivers. Just remember to keep your eyes peeled when in for a consultation with Eric—you never know who might show up.

Vanda orchids and red magic roses from South America stand up to the bold black velvet appliquéd leaves of the white matte satin tablecloth. Black sandblasted glass chargers add glitz and serve as the perfect counterpoint to the centerpieces' vibrant, luxuriant petals.

Photograph by Ellice Schwartz

Photograph by Eric Buterbaugh

Photograph by Hugo Burnand

Photograph by Hugo Burnand

"Monochromatic arrangements make a stronger statement than the mixed-up, fruit salad look."

—Eric Buterbaugh

Right: In order to successfully pull off the waterfall affect, we wired orange mokara orchids with steelgrass and let them cascade down from a plump orb of pink phalaenopsis orchids and tangerine roses. The whimsy of the floral arrangements was balanced by classic heavy silver charger plates and ornately scrolled flatware.

Facing page top: "Romantic" was the magic word for an intimate wedding in Parrot Cay in the Turks and Caicos Islands. Crystal candle globes sat atop specially made bevel-edge mirrors, letting the flickering light reflect even more. To create depth, we outfitted a handful of trees in the distance with white lanterns and twinkle lights, and placed rings of flowers surrounding glass bubble bowls and floating candles inside the pool. Each flower bouquet was made from singular ingredients: all roses or strictly freesias or only peonies.

Facing page bottom: How many people does it take to hand-string a ceiling-full of white cymbidium orchids? A lot! It took roughly 60 of my staff to assemble and hang each blossom from the erected birch branches, but the effect was akin to a fairytale. The tables had to be very narrow in order to fit all the guests, so the only tabletop adornments were crystal dishes containing floating cymbidium buds. Since the tables were mirrored, not only were the floating flowers reflected but the thousands of orchids dangling above were as well.

Photograph by Jennifer Roper

views

To get the best results from your floral designer, trust them enough to leave them alone. After collaborating with you to develop the concept, artists need room to experiment and flourish, and too many visits and suggestions after that can sap the energy and confuse the vision. Let your designer do what they do best, and what they produce will often end up being more than you ever imagined.

REVELRY

Edgardo Zamora's background is in fashion design—he had his own line of prêt a porter with retail stores in South America by the time he reached his mid-twenties. But he switched gears when he created the event design company Revelry with the help of his dear friend Bernie Neal. Revelry started out working on big projects in association with Along Came Mary, Sacks Productions, Ambrosia, Colin Cowie, and Sequoia Productions. At its start, Revelry was known for events like the Academy Awards® Governors Ball, film premieres, and high-profile fashion shows. But as the industry changed so did Revelry, and now its dazzling designs wow seen-it-all celebrities at weddings and social events.

Three years after he moved from Barcelona to Los Angeles and started his own event design company, Edgardo received a visit from his 11-year-old niece, Romina. The little girl spent a month helping him cut fabric, paint props, and ready decorations before returning home to Argentina, where she told her mother, "I want to work with my uncle when I get older." After graduating from a school geared toward future architects and interior designers, Romina Manolio is now Edgardo's partner and right-hand woman at Revelry, handling its biggest accounts like Mindy Weiss Party Consultants and working alongside lead event designers Matias Doorn and Oscar Cervantes. Edgardo has seen his designs replicated all over the world, but still insists that imitation is truly the sincerest form of flattery. He uses those occasions as motivation to reinvent himself and Revelry, consistently providing inspiration for new talent in the industry.

The top hat and round circulation benches from our Tufted collection were combined with floating organza, an Italian chiffon wall, and double-pile white angora carpet to create a welcoming, sexy space where the newlyweds and their guests could relax in chic comfort. The gorgeous orchid arrangements designed by Yvonne Van Pelt of Empty Vase delighted the bride and provided another textural layer.

Photograph by Nadine Froger Photography

Photograph by Nadine Froger Photography

Photograph by Eric Bertholet

Photograph by Nadine Froger Photography

Photograph by Nadine Froger Photography

"Every event needs to have the 'wow' effect."

—Edgardo Zamora

Right: The transformation of The Beverly Hills Hotel's Crystal Ballroom began with over 5,000 crystals cascading from the ceiling over the dance floor. Custom wallcoverings, tablecloths made with two layers of silk and finished by hand, and specially made chair covers for the existing hotel ballroom chairs turned the room into a whole other world.

Facing page top left: A stretch satin ceiling, custom-made black leather booths, and white leather walls embodied Art Deco ambience for the more than 800 guests celebrating the opening of the new L.A.P.D. headquarters, a look created by our own Matias Doorn and Mystika Garcia from Special Occasions. The crystal and chrome chandeliers, so integral in establishing the right atmosphere, were crafted by our team in East Los Angeles and not in China.

Facing page top right: We designed a cocktail event for the opening of the Hollywood Bowl's summer season, creating an incredible visual sensation for the guests with the orange spandex and sand organic drapes and our Ibiza furniture collection.

Facing page bottom left: Our team designed and produced every aspect of an event inspired by Old Havana decadence, from the hand-painted floor and hand-painted ceiling to the custom-made arches all finished by hand. It takes a very dedicated and talented team to pull off the events we do, and we love to work in conjunction with other event specialists. Marianne Weiman Nelson from Special Occasions designed the beautiful rock crystal chandeliers that illuminated the evening.

Facing page bottom right: We are honored to annually do the opening season gala for the Los Angeles Philharmonic, and one year we created a modern French ambience by mixing our oversized French mirrors with modern pieces. An incredible tabletop design by Nancy Kaye of Mark's Garden gave a twist to the formal crystal candelabras we're all used to seeing.

Photograph by Nadine Froger Photography

views

When I was a toddler, I would constantly rearrange my mother's furniture while she was out. Even back then I knew I would work in design! Now I keep a pen and pad of paper next to my bed, because ideas often come to me while I'm dreaming. When inspiration starts flowing like water at Niagara Falls, you have to write it all down—you never know what might be perfect for an event later on.

TOWN & COUNTRY EVENT RENTALS

RICHARD LOGUERCIO

You have to really love a business for it to draw you out of retirement, a fact that's not lost on Richard LoGuercio. After founding Classic Party Rentals in 1981 and building it into something of an empire, he sold it after 18 years. Retired at 45, Richard filled his days with volunteer work, taking care of his daughters, and learning how to build furniture. But he couldn't ignore the love he still had for the event rental business. What started as a part-time job in high school has grown into not one but two extremely successful companies; now, with Town & Country, Richard is working his magic on L.A.'s celebration circuit once more.

Town & Country has only been in business since 2005, but Richard's wealth of rentals knowledge goes back more than 40 years. His employees, many of whom were the driving force behind getting him back on the scene, share a similar enthusiasm and expertise, especially vice president Chris Mackey and operations manager Wayne Tay.

A self-professed "shopaholic," Richard travels the world acquiring a wide range of quality, trendsetting pieces. Everything from modular furniture to Moroccan-inspired flatware ends up in his 105,000-square-foot warehouse, where it is meticulously cared for. And if a host desires something a little more custom, Town & Country's fully equipped woodworking and metal welding shops can create or modify practically anything. Richard's passion for his work is obvious, otherwise he wouldn't be here—again.

Besides staples like chairs and tables, our inventory for outdoor parties encompasses everything from propane patio heaters to artificial hedges. A lot of times our topiary trees and other greenery end up looking better than the real thing!

Photograph by Line 8 Photography

Photograph by Wally Skalij

Photograph by Robert Cruzen

"Rentals shouldn't look rented. They should be pieces you would be proud to display in your own home."
—Richard LoGuercio

Right: Items like the candle wall and Florenzia sofa and chairs blur the line between rental and décor. When paired with the Maria Teresa black chandelier and Soho Cabana tent, the effect is that of an exclusive garden party.

Facing page: Some things, like the spacey, George Jetson-esque Panton chairs, I see while I'm traveling and just have to buy. Other pieces we make in-house, like translucent bars and furniture or Plexiglas and steel room dividers.

Photograph courtesy of Town & Country Event Rentals

views

A party is more fun when you're moving around. It's smart to have a wide variety of seating available for your guests, but it's even smarter to get them up and mingling. Create a couple of different areas that are easy to maneuver in and out of; that way your guests are encouraged to circulate and meet new people. Nothing kills a party quicker than making everybody feel trapped.

WILDFLOWER LINEN
YOUNGSONG MARTIN

Even as a child, Youngsong Martin was known for her keen style sense and passion for dressing with flair. Those instincts, and formal design school training, led to her successful career as a designer and nationwide marketer of namesake lines of upscale women's apparel. Then one day, Youngsong volunteered to help plan a niece's wedding. Unable to find suitable table linen rentals, she tapped her design expertise and knack for entertaining to craft just the right look for her niece's nuptials.

The satisfaction Youngsong derived from that experience soon inspired Wildflower Linen, which she founded in 2001 to showcase her innovative lines of designer table linens and chair covers for event rentals. That new career direction immediately brought Youngsong critical acclaim from noted event planners, celebrity caterers, and wedding hosts.

Since Wildflower Linen's inception, Youngsong has redefined the rental linen field with her company's couture quality and attention to customer care. Meanwhile, she launched four design showrooms throughout California and became a prestigious provider nationwide and abroad.

In addition to lavish weddings and large-scale society and corporate banquets, Wildflower Linen creations have been featured at the post-Oscars Governors® Ball and *Vanity Fair* afterparties, aboard charter yachts, in noted resorts and country clubs, at several presidential library events, even at the gala party for a DreamWorks premiere at the Venice Film Festival in Italy. However, Wildflower's extensive inventory of fashion-forward and traditional event décor has attracted hosts of even the most intimate of functions.

I require that each item in Wildflower Linen's distinctive Isabella line be hand-sewn to ensure the highest quality. The subtle textures of the ruffles add allure to the soft, neutral color palette.

Photograph by Barnet Photography

Photograph by Triple Cord Photography

Photograph by Aaron Delesie

Photograph courtesy of Grace Ormonde, Wedding Style magazine

Photograph courtesy of YWD magazine

"Live life courageously and step outside your comfort zone; I've found that's the only way to grow as a designer."

—Youngsong Martin

Right: Events can take on lives of their own, sometimes becoming fairytales of sorts with endless possibilities. This design took nautical and aquatic themes to another level, adding hints of "legends of the seas" fantasy. I evoked mermaids and magical underseas settings with the help of kelp accents and coral-like embellishments.

Facing page top left: In a break with tradition, I went to opposite ends of the design spectrum to marry rich dupioni silk with shiny leather floral appliqués, imparting a feminine, sophisticated look.

Facing page top right: Inspired by Dale Chihuly's blown-glass creations, I gave my Lilybelle line of chair covers a transparent, delicate floral effect that dazzles party guests.

Facing page bottom left: Color plays an indispensable role in any event's overall look, so I used multiple complementary tones to give an alfresco wedding a post-impressionistic feel.

Facing page bottom right: Like the apparel world's "little black dress" fashion staple, my design for this engagement party's chair covers has a chic, tailored simplicity that complements the understated table linens.

Photograph by Imagery Immaculate

views

Wildflower Linen's team emphasizes choice in catering to hosts' tastes and objectives. Event planners are encouraged to give free rein to their imaginations by exploring the breadth of our exclusive fabrics and styles to make their functions memorable. Party hosts should think of design vendors as their partners and collaborators.

Eat, Drink &

ALONG CAME MARY

MARY MICUCCI

Most people don't realize it, but the modern movie premiere as we know it today was originally inspired by spinach. When the Robin Williams film "Popeye" was set to debut in 1980, Paramount Pictures wanted to move away from the traditional hotel setting and throw a party unlike any Hollywood had ever seen before. They called on Mary Micucci to produce the unprecedented event. Known as "Hollywood's original catereress," Mary's passion for food and superb hostess skills revolutionized and in many ways created the party planning industry we know today.

With indispensable help from her vice president of catering and executive chef Bill Starbuck and executive pastry chef Eddie Cooper—known affectionately around the kitchen as "Chef Bill" and "Sweet Eddie"—Mary has built what originally started out as an all-female bartending company into a firm capable of all design, catering, and event logistics. Along Came Mary has catered and produced thousands of events for the corporate, entertainment, and private sectors, accumulating an unmatched wealth of knowledge.

A fundamental pillar of the company's success lies in its integrity and ethical values. Staff members are proud to stand behind their work, and that in turn produces consummate quality. Mary also insists on keeping her company as eco-conscious as possible while giving back to the community. She obtains much of her food from local, sustainable sources, and each year she supports major events for the National Resource Defense Council, Pediatric AIDS Foundation, and UCLA School of Medicine. What did Hollywood do before Mary came along?

We really excel at themed parties, and the premiere for "Lara Croft: Tomb Raider" provided so many creative elements from the movie to work with. An Asian dim sum buffet, featuring tantalizing shumai and spring rolls, was one of many grouped in front of a dramatic rising Buddha.

Photograph by Mark Elkins

Photograph by Mark Elkins

Photograph by 2me Studios

Above: Constantly coming up with new ways to serve classic dishes is a fun but never-ending experiment. Chef Bill created a cubed heirloom tomato salad with Burrata cheese and microgreens, drizzled with herb oil and balsamic syrup, delivering explosive taste in an intriguing, unexpected package.

Facing page: It's always tricky at a bar mitzvah to come up with creative, fresh ideas, because these kids are on a mitzvah circuit and go to so many events throughout the year. You need to stay one step ahead of the trends, and we really did by filling Mac computers with candy, using contemporary furniture pieces, and employing a green, yellow, and blue color palette that brought vibrancy and energy, especially since everything else was white and black.

"We're constantly challenged to come up with new ideas, stay with the trends, and create our own."

—Mary Micucci

Photograph by 2me Studios

Above: Another of Chef Bill's delicious creations, the rack of lamb and lamb loin with root purée and asparagus tips rests on a plate that is very simple and uncluttered. The play of the feminine red roses against the bold, more masculine linen comes together in a sophisticated, almost playful way.

Left: The table has an eclectic style, with different flatware at each setting, different chargers, various specialty glassware, and custom specialty linens—all elements meant to reflect the style of the host's home.

Facing page top: Held every 18 months as a fundraiser for the UCLA School of Medicine, the Millennium Ball was put together on a sound stage at a movie studio lot. I've always been very taken with how the architecture of the wall panel behind the guest seating plays off the angles and shapes of the phalaenopsis orchid adorning the table.

Facing page bottom: Black cod on potato purée with a spaghetti of vegetables, garnished with crispy matchstick leeks is such a light, fresh dish.

Photograph courtesy of Classic Party Rentals

Photograph by Mark Elkins

"Food is not a serious matter; it's a fun and passionate experience."
—Mary Micucci

Photograph by 2me Studios

Photograph by Line 8 Photography

Photograph by Line 8 Photography

"To see a naked room transform itself into something so glorious that it takes your breath away—that's the most exciting thing to me."

—Mary Micucci

Above: 2005 was the first year we produced the Grammy Celebration at the Los Angeles Convention Center; formerly, the event had been held at the Biltmore Hotel, which was much more compact with more intimate ballrooms. But this space was nearly the size of three football fields, so we knew it was important for décor elements—such as the cone chandeliers—to be absolutely massive! They lit up and changed color, so the environment of the room could really transform very easily.

Facing page: Each event has its own vibe, and everything from the décor to the presentation to the tiniest details should reflect that.

Previous pages: The way the gold and silver played off of each other, the shimmering linens, the white, modern centerpiece arrangements, the lighting, and the black chandeliers gave Petree Hall at the Los Angeles Convention Center a very elegant, 1950s supper club feel. The event honored Berry Gordy, founder and pioneer of Motown Records, plus celebrated the 50th anniversary of the Grammys, hence all of the golden touches.

Photograph by 2me Studios

Photograph by 2me Studios

Photograph by Line 8 Photography

Photograph by 2me Studios

Photograph by 2me Studios

Photograph by 2me Studios

Photograph by 2me Studios

"When the final touches are put on the party, the end result is always so amazing."

—Mary Micucci

Right: Shaved fennel tossed in a vinaigrette, then composed with micro parsley, summer plums, and capers all in a circular presentation gives the first course plum salad so much movement.

Facing page top left and bottom right: I'm always amazed and charmed at the delightful dessert creations Eddie Cooper comes up with. Ginger fig cake and a pear surprise are fines examples of his creativity.

Facing page top right: Interior designer and socialite Elsie de Wolfe, also known publicly as Lady Mendl, served as inspiration for a Cartier event. Dubbed America's first decorator, her style was to rid spaces of Victorian clutter, opening up rooms and introducing soft, warm colors and a bit of 18th-century French elegance.

Facing page bottom left: Ralph Rucci is a New York City-based fashion designer who established his label and independently owned company, Chado Ralph Rucci, in 1994. Chado is the name of an ancient Japanese ceremony involving 331 steps for preparing, serving, and drinking tea. He felt this discipline and attention to detail aligned with the philosophy he wanted to pursue in design. During the opening event for an exhibition of his clothing at the Phoenix Art Museum, we very much tried to incorporate the concepts of respect, tranquility, grace, and integrity into the event décor and design. Everything had really clean, graceful lines, with a slightly Asian feel.

Photograph by 2me Studios

views

I come from a long line of great Italian cooks, where every dinner was such a delicious occasion and every holiday was a glorious celebration. Entertaining doesn't have to be intimidating—keep it simple and focused and let it be the backdrop to enjoy the most important part of the event: your guests.

Wolfgang Puck Catering

Barbara Brass

Over the course of his career, Wolfgang Puck has evolved from a young, talented chef training in Europe to the head of a culinary brand that includes restaurants, consumer products, a television show, and a catering company. Puck's legendary success is grounded in his genuine hospitality and his passion for showcasing the simple goodness of food. Known for using the highest quality ingredients, which are ethical, seasonal, and sustainable, Wolfgang's signature cuisine celebrates flavor and texture without relying on heavy sauces or extraneous preparation. Since opening his landmark Hollywood restaurant, Spago, in 1982, the renowned chef's friendly demeanor and obvious joy for what he does continues to radiate throughout his empire, drawing like-minded professionals such as Barbara Brass, the vice president of catering sales, to his loyal team.

In 1998, after years of requests from loyal restaurant patrons, Wolfgang Puck Catering was established as a way to bring the chef's signature flair for fine dining to the event scene. The company has cemented its sterling reputation as the caterer for, among others, the post-Oscars Governors Ball, the Grammy Awards Post Celebration, and the Film Independent Spirit Awards, not to mention countless movie premieres.

Whether the guest list is for 10 or 5,000, in your home or at an iconic cultural center, the experience will always include the same attention to detail and remarkable level of freshness and creativity that can be found at any of Wolfgang's restaurants.

Our innovative presentation and flawless service is our signature. A fish becomes a work of art when the skeleton is creatively displayed atop a Dover sole with fava beans and artichokes.

Photograph courtesy of Wolfgang Puck Catering

Photograph courtesy of Wolfgang Puck Catering

Photograph courtesy of Wolfgang Puck Catering

Photograph courtesy of Wolfgang Puck Catering

Photograph courtesy of Wolfgang Puck Catering

Hors d'oeuvres like watermelon cubes with French feta and tarragon balsamic syrup; baby artichokes stuffed with shrimp, breadcrumbs, and lemon aioli; and baby beets with Burrata cheese and edible flowers are a feast for the eyes and mouth. Pomegranate-glazed short ribs with wasabi spaetzle give an unexpected kick to the cocktail hour.

"It's simple: food doesn't need to be fussed with if it's great to begin with."
—Barbara Brass

Photograph courtesy of Wolfgang Puck Catering

"Celebrate life through good food and good company."

—Wolfgang Puck

Roasted bass aqua pazza, which translates literally to "crazy water" in Italian, is a simple, flavorful dish made with olive oil and cherry tomatoes. Two distinctly different ways to serve fresh fish include spicy seafood paella or crispy potato pancakes topped with caviar and a mixture of smoked salmon and sturgeon.

Photograph courtesy of Wolfgang Puck Catering

Photograph courtesy of Wolfgang Puck Catering

Photograph courtesy of Wolfgang Puck Catering

Photograph courtesy of Wolfgang Puck Catering

Photograph courtesy of Wolfgang Puck Catering

Spicy tuna tartare in sesame miso cones are our signature. If you see them being passed, you know you're at a Wolfgang Puck event. The stacked tomato and mozzarella salad is striking in its presentation, while haricots verts salad with toasted pine nuts, goat cheese, and basil vinaigrette is a sophisticated take on the traditional salad.

Photograph courtesy of Wolfgang Puck Catering

"We really live Wolfgang's philosophy by treating everyone like a guest in our home."

—Barbara Brass

Left and facing page top: Whether your guests are adventurous—seafood ceviche shooters—or more conventional—mini-Kobé cheeseburgers—we put our spin on everything we serve.

Facing page bottom left: Black truffle chicken pot pie was a star at the 82nd Academy Awards® Governors Ball.

Facing page bottom right: Roasted filet mignon with potato leek galette, sautéed spinach, and roasted vegetables is a perennial crowd-pleaser.

Photograph courtesy of Wolfgang Puck Catering

Photograph courtesy of Wolfgang Puck Catering

Photograph courtesy of Wolfgang Puck Catering

Photograph courtesy of Wolfgang Puck Catering

Photograph courtesy of Wolfgang Puck Catering

Photograph courtesy of Wolfgang Puck Catering

Photograph courtesy of Wolfgang Puck Catering

"Cook from the heart and with love."
—Wolfgang Puck

Right: Wolfgang Puck is known worldwide as the masterful yet friendly face of his brand.

Facing page: Four sweet ways to end the night: a chocolate box filled with milk chocolate and orange mousse with candied oranges; a delicate chocolate teardrop with white chocolate mousse and Queen Anne cherries; a s'mores parfait; and our decadent chocolate chocolate profiteroles.

Photograph courtesy of Wolfgang Puck Catering

views

Our job is more than just showing up with a truckload of food. We take the time to build relationships with our hosts, and often we end up being there for each milestone they celebrate. Some hosts consult us for kitchen advice when they build a new house, and may even incorporate a catering-friendly kitchen designed to our specifications into their home. Following Wolfgang's lead, we build loyal relationships with our hosts and often share a lifetime of events.

GOOD GRACIOUS! EVENTS
PAULINE PARRY

Pauline Parry knows so much about being a hostess, you could say she wrote the book on it. *Food Fun Love*, written in 2009, shares recipes and delicious food from some of her favorite parties. But to get the Pauline Parry experience in person, you only have to call Good Gracious! Events and let them take the reins.

Pauline worked in hotel restaurant management in her native England before moving to Southern California with her husband. Pauline set about beginning her new life by arranging fabulous soirées and entertaining new friends. Only after those friends began suggesting that she should make a career out of her party skills did Pauline consider opening her own business. Since she formed Good Gracious! in 1986, Pauline has been diligent about ensuring each celebration she works on reflects each and every one of her clients' personal zest for life and passion for food.

The importance of teamwork at Good Gracious! is immediately apparent: most of the staff has been there for years, including executive chef Margarita Hernandez and award-winning chef de cuisine Joanne Purnell. This fun, focused business atmosphere has resulted in hundreds of industry awards, but the true measure of their success can be found in each of their marvelous events.

Every woman deserves to be a queen for the day, especially on her birthday. After enjoying cocktails in Santa Monica, the 150 guests were swept into 70 black limousines bearing diplomat's flags and police escorts to take them to downtown Los Angeles. As they were entering the gilded, turn-of-the-century ballroom, each guest was formally introduced to "the queen" before discovering a personalized crest waiting on their dinner plate.

Photograph by John Reiff Williams

Photograph by Will Henshall, Brilliant Studios.LA

"Parties are about filling lives with food, fun, and love."

—Pauline Parry

Photograph by Will Henshall, Brilliant Studios.LA

Photograph by Todd Johnson Photography

Photograph by B & B Photography

Photograph by Todd Johnson Photography

Whether it's a promotional event, a wedding, or a garden party, enchanting touches such as bold centerpieces and hanging jewels make a memorable impression. There are so many unique and fun ways to present food. A raised glass platform gives the illusion that a wedding cake is floating over a field of ruffled roses, while library shelves find a new purpose displaying appetizers and "books" customized for the party.

Photograph by Will Henshall, Brilliant Studios.LA

Photograph by Marianne Lozano Photography

"The perfect party happens when all the elements work together in harmony."

—Pauline Parry

Nothing pleases me more than working in conjunction with other terrific vendors. At an outdoor event we dubbed the "Leather and Lace" party, Rrivre Works, Classic Party Rentals, Chameleon Chairs, Millie Fiori Floral, The Lighter Side Lighting, and Wildflower Linen each demonstrated why they're the best at what they do, making the overall effect magnificent. For our part, we began the evening with five food and beverage hors d'oeuvre pairings, serving dishes that normally aren't seen during cocktail hour, such as paella cake with grilled shrimp and berry sangria.

Photograph by Marianne Lozano Photography

Photograph by Marianne Lozano Photography

Photograph by Marianne Lozano Photography

Photograph by Will Henshall of Brilliant Studios.LA

Photograph by Will Henshall, Brilliant Studios.LA

Photograph by Will Henshall, Brilliant Studios.LA

Photograph by John Reiff Williams

"Creativity is all about opening your mind up to the possibilities."
—Pauline Parry

Right: The yellow beets tower stuffed with basil pesto chevre cheese and topped with a crispy basil leaf is a versatile dish. Depending on its size, it can be served as an appetizer, as part of a plated meal, or beside a salad or panini.

Facing page top left: Fish and chips served with mushy peas is a nod to my homeland, but its contemporary presentation, with the stacked fries and tartar sauce in a wooden box, adds sophistication.

Facing page top right: Our alternative to a doily is a piece of parchment paper bearing words that evoke the spirit of the event. When placed beneath a signature dessert, like our peach crème brûlée with raspberry compote, it provides a fun, personalized touch.

Facing page bottom: We're very aware that the details make the difference. Our butternut squash soup starts out as a bowl sprinkled with the nuggets, then waiters appear to pour piping hot carafes of the soup and garnish it with a tied knot of chive. We'll serve salmon wound into a circle atop grainy mustard mashed potatoes and finished off with a Chinese bean knot to create visual interest.

Photograph by Will Henshall, Brilliant Studios LA

views

Food, fun, and love are the cornerstones of my business and my life. Every host should remember, amidst all the hustle and decision-making and anxiety, that these three ideals are really what it's all about.

CRÈME DE LA CRÈME

MARK MISKIEWICZ

Hosting a party in a ballroom or a private home—where's the challenge in that? During his more than three decades of experience, chef Mark Miskiewicz has prepared delectable meals aboard private yachts, in remote locations, and with more than 45,000 hungry mouths waiting beside a buffet. Some might call what he specializes in "extreme catering," but Mark considers it just another exciting aspect of the job he loves. Since forming Crème de la Crème in 1989, Mark has since produced over 4,000 events and concocted some of the most memorable and mouthwatering dishes for celebrities and regular folk alike.

He and his team, including his office manager and right-hand woman Jennifer Wilson, can create five-star gourmet meals at nearly any location and utilizing any level of budget. The secret to their extremely tasty success is that they hand-make everything, from appetizers to desserts and every morsel in between. Next, personal attention to each plate produces flawless results. Plates emerge from the kitchen sizzling hot, reaching the table with alacrity seldom found at banquets. Mark likens the experience to dining at the world's best restaurant, except that the portability of catering makes taking that restaurant-like feel anywhere in the world possible. The term crème de la crème is known to mean superlative, the very best, and it's with that description in mind that Mark approaches every event.

We are extremely proud of our presentation skills and always try to find new and inventive ways to display our dishes. An Israeli buffet showcased our own shawarma, gyros, and marinated rotisserie meats amongst Middle Eastern pottery and grainy burlap sacks.

Photograph by Mark Miskiewicz

Photograph by Pat Rogers

"Catering tends to present more options than you would find at a fine restaurant."

—Mark Miskiewicz

Photograph by Pat Rogers

Photograph by Pat Rogers

Photograph by Pat Rogers

Photograph by Pat Rogers

Above and right: Whether it's hors d'oeuvres, a first course, or the final spoonful of a dessert, we don't let a single detail slip. Each item receives individual attention before being presented to a guest.

Facing page: Decades in the business have honed our collaboration skills, and we find that working with other vendors is a terrific way to pool creative ideas and deliver a table or buffet that is striking, memorable, and eye-catching.

Photograph by Pat Rogers

Photograph by Tony Sanders

Photograph by Tony Sanders

Photograph by Tony Sanders

Photograph by Pat Rogers

"This profession encompasses so many skill sets, but it's the variety that keeps it challenging."

—Mark Miskiewicz

"Personalization" and "customization" are the two magic words. We of course have sample menus, but we're more than happy to accommodate special regional and dietary requests. If a particular side dish holds special meaning or every item needs to adhere to a theme, by all means let us know and we'll do everything we can to fulfill the dream.

Photograph by Pat Rogers

views

When comparing caterers, make sure you're matching apples to apples. Does the bid include staffing? If so, how many? What else is included—or will it cost extra later? Don't just look at the bottom line; make sure you know what you're really looking for and that you're honest with yourself about your budget.

SERVES YOU RIGHT! CATERING

MICHELE GAN

For some, a career is simply an avenue to earn a living and provide for a desired lifestyle. Not so for Michele Gan. Although her journey in the culinary and service industry began as a young teenager garnishing plates in a local restaurant, her work in the culinary arts has become her heart's passion.

With a conviction that food should taste the same whether it's served for 10 people or 1,000 people, Michele founded Serves You Right! Catering and determined that the way to achieve consistently delicious food was in the people as much as it was in the ingredients. She believes it's important for her employees to understand their value and roles so they can share in the success of achieving flawless events. On the team is the executive chef, Mikell Varn, who has a natural talent for developing exceptional cuisines that satisfy the tastes of every event host and guest. With the combination of Mikell's talent in the kitchen and Michele's attention to detail, they have developed a strong bond and successful team.

That success has translated into preparing meals for numerous high-profile events including presidential dinners, museum openings, fashion events, and celebrity celebrations. One thing each fête has in common is Michele's ability to make the host feel comfortable knowing that the celebration is in her more-than-capable hands. Treating every host and guest with the same importance, Michele will not sleep until she knows that each detail and request has been fulfilled.

The setting for a culinary experience needs to be perfectly planned, down to the style and placement of silverware. Subtly integrating the client's logo into the table setting was the perfect way to incorporate branding into the VIP dinner.

Photograph by Paula Tripodi

Photograph by Serves You Right! Catering

"Creating and serving food is a craft of love."

—Michele Gan

Photograph by Serves You Right! Catering

Photograph by Robin Layton

We often receive inspiration from the surroundings for our cuisine and décor, whether the event is held in a lovely outdoor patio with long, clean lines mimicking the neighboring garden or poolside with umbrellas for shade amidst the bright spring colors. Likewise, at an evening dinner party on the beach, we designed a simple, elegant setting to allow the natural scene to exude its beauty.

Photograph by Robin Layton

Photograph by Robin Layton

Photograph by Robin Layton

Photograph by Robin Layton

Photograph by Serves You Right! Catering

"Overhandled food loses its natural beauty and taste."

—Michele Gan

Organic, seasonal food is at the heart of every dish we prepare. Even substituting one ingredient for something less fresh can have a tremendous impact on the taste and appearance. From New Zealand green-lipped mussels accompanying a paella dinner to an heirloom tomato gazpacho served in a whimsical floral dish, every bite captures the flavor and essence of the season and region.

views

It's vital for the service staff members to understand that they are ambassadors of the catering company as well as the host, whether it be for a corporate event or a private, in-home function. If a catering staff member doesn't know what he or she is serving or provides unsatisfactory service, it can ruin not only the guests' experience, but the reputation of the host and caterer as well.

AN CATERING BY CRUSTACEAN

CATHERINE AN

In 2006, Catherine An infused her love of art and fashion into the launch of An Catering, becoming known almost immediately as the go-to caterer for the Hollywood crowd. As a member of the An family, revered owners of what some say was the first Vietnamese restaurant in San Francisco and two outposts of the wildly popular Crustacean restaurant, Catherine's culinary pedigree speaks volumes. Helene An and her five daughters have been perfecting culinary excellence for over 40 years. Helene, matriarch and executive chef of all of the family's restaurants, spent much of her free time as a child in the kitchen with her family's three chefs of Chinese, French, and Vietnamese descent, absorbing their cultural differences and culinary techniques. This enabled her to develop her personal "Ying and Yang" culinary philosophy of healthy and balanced eating.

Rather than simply rely on a famous name, Catherine has worked hard to establish An Catering as a company admired for its mouthwatering food and chic presentation. An Catering's welcoming hospitality, unwavering sense of culinary creativity, and strong family bond make it a standout in the event world. Through her global travels, Catherine keeps An Catering innovative, fresh, and full of diverse flavors. Additionally, Catherine insists on only using the freshest, seasonally appropriate ingredients while striving to use the greenest alternatives possible.

Besides featuring the deliciously healthy cuisine of our mother, Helene, we also have an in-house visual designer, mixologist, and sommelier to ensure each event is flawlessly executed. Drinks like the Waterfall, a combination of vanilla vodka, peach schnapps, and white cranberry juice, and the Pink Lotus, a cocktail that is poured over cotton candy, evaporating the sugary strands as it fills the glass, are what help to make a memorable experience.

Photograph by Zen Todd

Photograph by Zen Todd

Photograph by Jessica Boone

Photograph by Jessica Boone

Photograph by Eric Raptosh

Photograph by Eric Raptosh

"Warm hospitality is important to us. Whether the count is 20 or 2,000, people should feel like they're dining in their own home."

—Catherine An

By opening a catering division, we were able to bring our "Secret Kitchen" to other locations. The Secret Kitchen is a smaller, closed-off part of the Crustacean kitchen where only family members and longtime employees who have worked with the family over 10 years are allowed to enter. It's there that we make the dishes that have become our signatures, like the famous garlic noodles, tiger prawns, and Dungeness crab. We also have an extensive understanding of vegetarian, vegan, and organic diets, and have even introduced a molecular menu.

Photograph by Zen Todd

views

When my mother first came to America she used a combination of persistence and hard work to turn a nondescript deli into the San Francisco landmark Thanh Long is today. Today, I combine my mother's Old World hospitality with a forward-thinking perspective to give guests an incredible experience.

CAKE DIVAS

LEIGH GRODE | JOAN SPITLER

The basic ingredients for a cake are flour, sugar, salt, butter, baking powder, eggs, and milk. But when the Cake Divas of Los Angeles make a cake, sometimes you wonder if they haven't sprinkled a little fairy dust in the bowl for good measure. Leigh Grode and Joan Spitler have been partners in baking since 1998, when they realized their artistic vision and culinary talents could create magic in the kitchen. Since then their fame has only grown, with appearances on the national television shows "Amazing Wedding Cakes," "Ultimate Cake Off," "Platinum Weddings," and quite a few others.

Known for their lavish wedding cakes and far-out artwork cakes, Leigh and Joan have no problem bringing a taste of theatricality to the table. They often produce cakes that are seen in movies and television shows, and are always on the cutting edge of design trends. With backgrounds that encompass art and filmmaking, they are right at home in L.A.'s glamorous entertainment scene, but can also be flown around the world at a moment's notice to bake a delicious treat for a mysterious superstar.

But famous or not, everyone who comes to Cake Divas is enfolded into a collaborative process that always produces astounding, personalized, oftentimes quirky, and always mouthwatering results. It's why Leigh and Joan decided to become Divas in the first place: to add a bit more sugar to the world.

Hundreds of handmade sugar pearls in varying sizes give a wedding cake opulence, especially with the contrast of the soft detail against the sharper squares of the tiers.

Photograph by Robert Evans

Photograph by Ultimate Image Photography

Photograph by John Solano

Photograph by Leigh Grode

Photograph by Leigh Grode

"Be realistic, but don't lose that sense of fantasy."

—Leigh Grode

Inspiration can come from anywhere: a favorite flower, the draping of a gown, or the previously chosen motif for the invitations and décor. The materials help determine a cake's effect: fondant icing is ideal for echoing the folds of fabric, while buttercream icing provides a timeless, elegant look when paired with handmade sugar flowers.

Photograph by Dahl Photography

views

There are two kinds of cake decorators: the ones who will design based solely on their ideas and vision, and the ones who will really listen, discover your individuality, and create a cake unique to you that will surpass your wildest dreams. If someone is adamant in telling you how they think something should be done, take a step back and decide if you agree with them. If you don't, walk out the door.

Coast Catering by Barry Layne

BARRY LAYNE | JENNIFER LAYNE

Putting your name in a company's title is a bold decision, but Barry Layne happily stands behind his statement. More than just a name, Barry is often the first point of contact hosts have with Coast Catering. Knowing that you will be working directly with the owner himself provides a large degree of comfort, especially in an economic climate that has made people hesitant to loosen their purse strings. Besides collaborating side by side with hosts to design fully personalized menus and monitoring events on-site, Barry can often be found in the kitchen, working alongside his trusted team of chefs. To call Barry a hands-on owner would be an understatement; to call him dedicated would be just the beginning.

At 15, Barry was a hotel jack-of-all-trades, working every job from bell-hop to busboy. But it was the restaurant side he fell in love with, and that newfound passion for food quickly translated into positions at JC Resorts, Ventana Inn in Big Sur, the José Eber Salon Café, and Delicias in Rancho Santa Fe. It was during his 10-year stint as executive chef and assistant general manager at Delicias that Barry ventured into catering, and in 2005 he left to open his own company.

Although they have provided for guests numbering into the thousands, Barry and his wife Jennifer are careful not to spread themselves too thin. Impeccable attention to detail, as well as a versatile, gourmet style that has attracted foodies and celebrities alike, is what Coast Catering is known for.

A contemporary coastal grazing station showcases not only domestic and imported olives, cheeses, and meats, but also accompaniments we craft ourselves. Homemade fig and apricot jam and truffle- and lavender-infused honey complement the savory options, while grilled flatbread is just begging to be paired with our made-from-scratch hummus. We have cultivated relationships with private farms, local meat and fish companies, and other vendors to ensure that we're always starting with only the finest and freshest ingredients.

Photograph by Paul Barnett

Photograph courtesy of Coast Catering

Photograph courtesy of Coast Catering

Photograph by Boyd Harris

Photograph by Boyd Harris

Photograph by Philip DeFalco

"Getting the right professionals involved is the easiest way to make your event seamless."

—Barry Layne

Because of my restaurant background, I am constantly encouraging people to stop by and see how we're evolving. One way we've done that is by basing our company in a retail restaurant space. We serve lunch during the week with a menu that's constantly changing, not only with the seasons but with what we want to experiment with next. We also host themed dinners, nights where we play with Asian fusion dishes or design courses based on a selection of wines, beers, or even scotches being served. Besides inviting people who may not be familiar with Coast to try us out, our restaurant provides a great opportunity to keep our skills fresh.

views

When you're in the midst of choosing a caterer, a tasting is a terrific way to gauge if their style matches up with yours, how they handle special requests, and how they present themselves. However tempting it might be to try out 8 or 10 different companies, limit tastings to only your top three. Any more and important details can get lost. Do your research, collect referrals, and have an initial meeting before scheduling a tasting. By the time the fork reaches your lips, you should have a pretty good idea of which caterer will be the best match for you.

Capturing the

WAYNE FOSTER MUSIC & ENTERTAINMENT
WAYNE FOSTER | MARIN FOSTER

A Swarovski crystal-pavéd grand piano? Of course, anything is possible! Wayne Foster Music & Entertainment takes requests of all sorts in order to create the right ambience and keep guests uplifted, entertained, and fully engaged throughout the evening.

Consistently developing new talent and adding the latest hits to its extremely diverse repertoire, the company has been making people smile for more than half a century. And it all began with two teenagers—Marin and Wayne Foster, then sweethearts, now spouses and the proud parents and grandparents of talented musicians. They saw an opportunity, proved themselves, and quickly became the preeminent source for the best vocalists, instrumentalists, and dancers. Today, the Foster troupe is nearly 500 strong, and it's from that wonderful pool of talent that performers are hand-selected for each event. Whether the occasion calls for a soloist, a string ensemble, a full dance orchestra, or a large group of musical geniuses to electrify the stage, the company is happy to help—and it's done so from its headquarters in Southern California, across the country, and around the world.

Experts in the science of celebration, the performers are known for their extraordinary talent and also for their professionalism. It's a given that anyone invited to be part of the extended Foster family has a great attitude, a pleasant appearance, and an innate eagerness to grow as an artist. Trends in the music industry are always on the move, and so are the performers of Wayne Foster Music & Entertainment.

Show tunes and movie scores are great during dinner because they encourage conversation and offer a nice balance of sophistication and fun. While the flow of music is continuous, we intentionally switch between genres and eras to keep guests engaged and entertained.

Photograph by John Solano

Photograph courtesy of Wayne Foster Music & Entertainment

Photograph courtesy of Wayne Foster Music & Entertainment

We love social music—all of it, every single genre. And because celebrations naturally include a potpourri of guests, it is best to perform a wide variety of music. Keeping our hosts' preferences in mind, we'll generally start out with a universal favorite like Sinatra or R&B sounds of Earth, Wind & Fire. As the event progresses, contemporary music is added to enhance the energy and keep the young and the young at heart engaged. During dinner, Andrea Bocelli's "The Prayer" usually elicits as great of a response as the music of Jason Mraz or Norah Jones, solidifying the concept that a variety of musical styles appeals to all.

"The only way to keep the energy level high is through continuous music—no intermissions, no breaks, just a pleasant flow from one song to the next."

—Wayne Foster

Photograph by Paul Barnett

Photograph by Boyd Harris

Photograph courtesy of Wayne Foster Music & Entertainment

Photograph courtesy of Wayne Foster Music & Entertainment

Photograph courtesy of Wayne Foster Music & Entertainment

"Concerts are about the performers, whereas parties are about the guests. Social music is wonderfully participatory in nature."

—Wayne Foster

Part of what makes our work so special is that we're running a family business. Each generation who joins the ranks becomes not just part of a company, but an integral part of a family legacy, an enterprise that represents the well-being of cherished loved ones. We take great pride in our musical art form, and it comes through in the level of thought and attention to detail that goes into every performance: the music as well as the staging, wardrobe, choreography, and set and lighting design. Sometimes our performers go on sabbatical to tour with celebrity stars and Broadway tours—that's how good they are—but they always come home.

Photograph courtesy of Wayne Foster Music & Entertainment

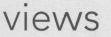

views

The relevance of appropriate musical entertainment at a philanthropic gala is of great significance. There are two main philosophies for running philanthropic events: Tug at people's heartstrings to make a donation obligatory or create a frame of mind that inspires benevolence and sharing. Clearly, we subscribe to the latter philosophy—our music always dwells on making people feel good. Over the years, we've had the opportunity to support a number of worthy causes through our brand of energizing and motivating performances with extraordinary results.

West Coast Music

JIM EPPOLITO

One thing Jim Eppolito has learned after decades in the event business is that the food can be delectable, the décor sublime, and the service impeccable, but if no one's enjoying the music then the party can't be considered a success. Luckily, as the owner of West Coast Music, Jim knows exactly how to remedy such a situation.

Since 1988, West Coast Music has been supplying Southern California with some of the most engaging live musical performances to be found anywhere. With seven bands and numerous specialty entertainers capable of performing anything from current pop hits to classic soul and Motown to elegant orchestras and everything in between, there's not much that West Coast Music can't do. With the help of his dedicated staff, Jim handles all the details to ensure that his musicians deliver award-winning performances at every event. West Coast Music develops the majority of its bands in-house, meaning it ultimately has more control over wardrobe choices, rehearsal time, and repertoire selections. As Jim sees it, this management is what makes his company special; with everyone working hard toward the same goal, the results are always spectacular.

With a client list that spans pop culture, professional sports, the film industry, award shows, and music industry legends, Jim is often considered the go-to guy for top-notch entertainment. After watching guests sway and bop when his performers take the stage, it's not hard to see why.

Nothing is set in stone; we can arrange a single guitarist or an entire 20-piece band, and even add on musicians if the event would benefit from a larger sound. It's all about determining what would provide the right tone and quality for the event.

Photograph by Jay Lawrence Goldman

Photograph by Sean Holt

Photograph by Sean Holt

Our performers are extremely diverse. In addition to "icon artists," who specialize in the songs of such idols as Frank Sinatra and Michael Bublé, we have bands that can switch from The Beatles to Rihanna and Coldplay with complete authenticity.

"Two days later, nobody is going to remember exactly what we played— they're going to remember the energy we created."

—Jim Eppolito

Photograph by John Solano

Photograph by John Solano

Photograph by John Solano

"Music is supposed to convey a mood. If it doesn't make you feel anything, it's just noise."

—Jim Eppolito

Right and facing page bottom: One of the benefits of having live performers is that they are very adept at gauging the energy of the crowd. Getting the guests more involved or mellowing them down so the bride and groom can share a special moment is a valuable skill.

Facing page top: Sometimes the addition of a "name" can provide that extra jolt of excitement to an event. We can help with selecting, acquiring, and booking a guest artist, and then completely coordinate their performance so that the host doesn't have to worry about a thing. In the past year alone, we've worked with over 100 celebrity musicians. Legendary performers such as Lionel Richie and Kenny "Babyface" Edmonds have given guests extremely memorable nights.

Photograph by John Solano

views

When choosing the types of music for your event, don't rely solely on your own preferences. Not only should you think about the mood you want to set, but it's wise to take into account the ages, backgrounds, and preferences of your guests. Nothing will elicit a better response than when the band strikes up the first few notes of a certain era's standard or a particular song that holds special meaning for those in attendance.

Aaron Delesie Photographer

AARON DELESIE

Aaron Delesie has never had a job that didn't involve photography. Whether working in a photo lab or apprenticing for the most renowned celebrity portrait photographers in the world, Aaron has had a camera in his hand ever since he was 17. Combine a talent and creative history like that with a photography degree from The Art Center College of Design in Pasadena, and the result is one of the most sought-after wedding and event photographers in the nation.

Running a truly boutique company—he accepts only 25 events a year—has given Aaron complete control over his work, something he takes great pride in. But his creative contributions don't stop once the party ends. Aaron works closely with each host to design and produce photography books that feature his exquisite images, expertly touched-up and arranged to convey the story of the event.

Transitioning from the carefully controlled environments of commercial still life to the ever-changing landscape of parties has given Aaron hard-won experience in all types of situations. His diverse background and technical finesse have prepared him to expect the unexpected. Juggling timelines and managing emotions are all par for the course during an event, but Aaron's affable demeanor and ability to go with the event's flow have proved invaluable over the years. It's something Aaron maintains can't be taught, only honed through time and experience. While his composure may be nearly impossible to rattle, the energy and vibrancy of life's most important moments certainly come through in his photographs.

A lot of people don't think of event photography as art, but that all depends on your definition. Most likely a bride's portrait or a candid from a party will never hang in a museum, but to the people I created them for, they're priceless.

Photograph by Aaron Delesie

Photograph by Aaron Delesie

Photograph by Aaron Delesie

Photograph by Aaron Delesie

Photograph by Aaron Delesie

Photograph by Aaron Delesie

"Photographs should tell the story of an event."

—Aaron Delesie

The absolute last thing I want hosts and guests to do is miss their party because they were having their picture taken. I shoot very fast for a number of reasons: large groups of people have shorter attention spans, you can get a better shot when someone has their defenses down, and it allows everyone to continue doing what they came to do—enjoy the occasion!

views

Everyone is photogenic, but most people aren't entirely comfortable in front of a camera. As a photographer, it's my job to describe to them what I'm doing and why, to talk them through the experience and help them relax. If someone feels awkward, then the photo will be awkward. You can't argue with people's perceptions about themselves, but you can change their minds by showing them a great photo.

ENTERTAINMENT PLUS PRODUCTIONS

DOUGLAS JOHNSON

How did a poor boy from Alabama grow up to enjoy both a successful performing career and his own full-service entertainment production company? By having charm and moxie to spare. Doug Johnson always had the showbiz bug, whether he was playing his church's piano, performing at Six Flags Over Georgia, dabbling in musical theater and ballet, or working in film and television. But a desire to choreograph and a realization that he had the skills and drive to form his own business led Doug to open Entertainment Plus Productions in the late 1990s. Now the company produces the prestigious New Year's Eve party at the Bellagio in Las Vegas, has its own show at the Rio Hotel and Casino, and has produced entertainment for international touring shows, movie premieres, celebrity shindigs, and corporate events, to name a few.

Whether salacious and tantalizing or conservative and family-friendly, Entertainment Plus Productions creates compelling live shows and entertainment that rely on spectacular costumes—some even designed by Bob Mackey—stunning lighting and visual effects, unique staging, and the industry's leading talent. Many members of the ensemble have been with Doug for years, but agent-sponsored auditions in L.A. help discover rising stars.

Knowing that performances can easily seem repetitive to those on the event circuit, Entertainment Plus constantly reworks, revamps, and updates its performances to deliver an unforgettable audience experience. Singers, dancers, impersonators, comics, musicians, gymnasts—each is an integral part of the Entertainment Plus family and works hard to make an event unique.

A cast of 60 sang and danced right up through the countdown at the Bellagio's New Year's Eve party. The finale involved 200 pounds of recycled plastic snowflakes, and because of its volume the performers didn't get a chance to rehearse with it beforehand. Luckily it all went off without a hitch, the effect was magical, and afterward 2,000 guests turned the elegant room into an all-out snowball fight.

Photograph by Curtis Dahl Photography

Photograph by Curtis Dahl Photography

Photograph by Serge Nikolich

Photograph by 2me Studios

Photograph by Curtis Dahl Photography

Photograph by Curtis Dahl Photography

"In the world of entertainment, never say never. What might sound crazy on paper could be the beginning of the most amazing performance."

—Douglas Johnson

Versatility is one of our greatest assets. We can do any style, genre, time period, or approach, and it's a thrill to explore something we've never encountered before. Something I've noticed over the years is how the energy of a room changes during and after a performance: people feel freer, more enthusiastic, and it's miraculous how an event can benefit from that newfound buoyancy.

Photograph by Mark Howell

views

I swore when I made the switch from actor to producer that I would never get "producer's syndrome" and forget how hard it is for the performers. I'm proud of my talented crew and treat them with the respect they deserve. Some may view what we do as silly fluff but we bring joy to people's lives, if even for a little bit, and that's important work.

JAY LAWRENCE GOLDMAN PHOTOGRAPHY

JAY LAWRENCE GOLDMAN

If you want to shoot portraits, technical savvy just isn't enough. You have to genuinely enjoy people—understanding their stories, appreciating their innate beauty, creating an artistic expression of who they are. A husband, father, teacher, painter, musician, blogger, gourmet chef, and regular guest photographer on "America's Next Top Model," Jay Goldman has a disarming quality that allows him to instantly connect with just about anyone.

For events, Jay appears on location quietly—sans intimidating amounts of photography luggage—and eases his way into each scene to capture meaningful moments throughout the day and evening. He's partial to artsy and unexpected shots but fully appreciates the breadth of photo-documentary work that is desired at family-oriented celebrations. After scouting out the perfect scene, his assistants will set up a studio-away-from-home so that when the time is right, Jay can assemble family and close friends for a quick session of perfectly lit, heirloom-quality portraits.

While he's certainly well-known for his wedding work, Jay has a wide variety of commissions; fine art photography, magazine work, and hip ad campaigns keep him busy and creatively stimulated. Jay has photographed subjects from the rich and famous to non-celebrities young and old, beautiful landscapes to real-world roughness, designer jewelry to stylized gummy bears. Jay is not afraid to have fun, to stretch himself creatively. And the trend continues to the fabulous post-production work he does in his digital darkroom: layering, texturing, colorizing, or whatever else will enhance the emotion his image seeks to evoke.

Technology is amazing in the possibilities it affords. Sometimes digital images almost feel too crisp and perfect. I've always had an affinity for the cinematographic quality of black and white film, and the ability to change any great shot to have that "look" is a creative jackpot.

Photograph by Jay Lawrence Goldman

Photograph by Jay Lawrence Goldman

Photograph by Jay Lawrence Goldman

Photograph by Jay Lawrence Goldman

Photograph by Jay Lawrence Goldman

"Great event photographs are not about luck, but about being prepared, aware, and focused. You have to put yourself in the right spot at the right time to capture those perfect moments. That comes with experience."

—Jay Lawrence Goldman

I love capturing the moment that a woman goes from fiancée to bride. There's a remarkable glow about the whole event, but those few minutes from veil to aisle are particularly special and need to be cherished. Instead of simply shooting at one location and then moving to another, I like to document the full journey to create a fluid story. Doing that requires thinking a few shots ahead and setting up the path, lighting, and angles so that photography opportunities happen naturally.

Photograph by Jay Lawrence Goldman

views

In order to stay fresh, you need to look for creative opportunities everywhere. I love balancing the Zen-like quality of studio work with the exciting whirlwind of events. They require such different approaches and exploring them makes me feel more complete as an artist.

INDEX

Art of Celebration

SOUTHERN CALIFORNIA TEAM

VICE PRESIDENT & SENIOR PUBLISHER: Carla Bowers

ASSOCIATE PUBLISHER: Andrea Burkhart

ASSOCIATE PUBLISHER: Valerie Serwer

SENIOR GRAPHIC DESIGNER: Emily A. Kattan

EDITOR: Lindsey Wilson

MANAGING PRODUCTION COORDINATOR: Kristy Randall

HEADQUARTERS TEAM

PUBLISHER: Brian G. Carabet

PUBLISHER: John A. Shand

EXECUTIVE PUBLISHER: Phil Reavis

PUBLICATION & CIRCULATION MANAGER: Lauren B. Castelli

GRAPHIC DESIGNER: Kendall Muellner

GRAPHIC DESIGNER: Paul Strength

MANAGING EDITOR: Rosalie Z. Wilson

EDITOR: Anita M. Kasmar

EDITOR: Jennifer Nelson

EDITOR: Sarah Tangney

PRODUCTION COORDINATOR: Drea Williams

PROJECT COORDINATOR: Laura Greenwood

TRAFFIC COORDINATOR: Brandi Breaux

ADMINISTRATIVE MANAGER: Carol Kendall

CLIENT SUPPORT COORDINATOR: Amanda Mathers

PANACHE PARTNERS, LLC

CORPORATE HEADQUARTERS

1424 GABLES COURT

PLANO, TX 75075

469.246.6060

www.panache.com

www.panachecelebrations.com

THE PANACHE COLLECTION

CREATING SPECTACULAR PUBLICATIONS FOR DISCERNING READERS

Dream Homes Series
An Exclusive Showcase of the Finest Architects, Designers and Builders

Carolinas
Chicago
Coastal California
Colorado
Deserts
Florida
Georgia
Los Angeles
Metro New York
Michigan
Minnesota
New England

New Jersey
Northern California
Ohio & Pennsylvania
Pacific Northwest
Philadelphia
South Florida
Southwest
Tennessee
Texas
Washington, D.C.

Spectacular Homes Series
An Exclusive Showcase of the Finest Interior Designers

California
Carolinas
Chicago
Colorado
Florida
Georgia
Heartland
London
Michigan
Minnesota
New England

Metro New York
Ohio & Pennsylvania
Pacific Northwest
Philadelphia
South Florida
Southwest
Tennessee
Texas
Toronto
Washington, D.C.
Western Canada

Perspectives on Design Series
Design Philosophies Expressed by Leading Professionals

California
Carolinas
Chicago
Colorado
Florida
Georgia
Great Lakes
Minnesota

New England
New York
Pacific Northwest
Southwest
Western Canada

Art of Celebration Series
The Making of a Gala

Chicago & the Greater Midwest
Georgia
New England
New York
Philadelphia
South Florida
Southern California
Southwest
Texas
Toronto
Washington, D.C.
Wine Country

Spectacular Wineries Series
A Captivating Tour of Established, Estate and Boutique Wineries

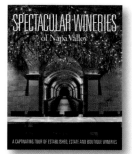

California's Central Coast
Napa Valley
New York
Sonoma County
Texas

Specialty Titles
The Finest in Unique Luxury Lifestyle Publications

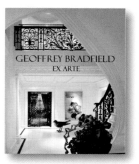

Cloth and Culture: Couture Creations of Ruth E. Funk
Distinguished Inns of North America
Extraordinary Homes California
Geoffrey Bradfield Ex Arte
Into the Earth: A Wine Cave Renaissance
Spectacular Golf of Colorado
Spectacular Golf of Texas
Spectacular Hotels
Spectacular Restaurants of Texas
Visions of Design

City by Design Series
An Architectural Perspective

Atlanta
Charlotte
Chicago
Dallas
Denver
Orlando
Phoenix
San Francisco
Texas

PanacheCelebrations.com
Where the Event Industry's Finest Professionals Gather, Share, and Inspire

Panache Celebrations

PanacheCelebrations.com overflows with innovative ideas from leading event planners, designers, caterers, and other specialists. A gallery of photographs and library of advice-oriented articles are among the comprehensive site's offerings.

Panache Partners, LLC   1424 Gables Court   Plano, Texas 75075   469.246.6060   www.panache.com